Essential Skills for Managers of Child-Centred Settings

Excellence in Childcare
Series Editor: Maureen Smith

This book is part of the Excellence in Childcare series. The series is designed to support students and NVQ candidates, practitioners, managers and trainers to develop their skills and offer a high quality service to children and families.

Books in the series are written by experts with many years' experience of and commitment to the childcare sector. As the sector grows and develops, there is a demand not only for more childcare provision, but for better quality provision. The sector now requires very well qualified, excellent practitioners who can support children's development through their work. The series aims to help new and established practitioners become confident, imaginative, excellent professionals.

Essential Skills for Managers of Child-Centred Settings

Emma Isles-Buck and Shelly Newstead

David Fulton Publishers

David Fulton Publishers
2 Park Square, Milton Park, Abingdon, Oxon OX14 4RN

270 Madison Avenue, New York, NY 10016

First published in Great Britain in 2003 by David Fulton Publishers
Transferred to digital printing

David Fulton Publishers is an imprint of the Taylor & Francis Group, an informa business

Copyright © Emma Isles-Buck and Shelly Newstead 2003

The right of the authors to be identified as the authors of this work has been asserted by them in accordance with the Copyright, Designs and Patents Act 1988.

British Library Cataloguing in Publication Data
A catalogue record for this book is available from the British Library.

ISBN 1 84312 034 8

Typeset by Servis Filmsetting Ltd, Manchester

Contents

Acknowledgements

Writing this book has been a culmination of experience gained through being managed ourselves by effective and ineffective managers, managing teams ourselves (both effectively and ineffectively!) and working with others to overcome the management skills gaps in the sector. We would like to thank sincerely the following practitioners for their support in taking time to read and comment on the chapters: Maureen Smith, Anne Kelly, Verona Beaumont, Maria White, Beverly Webb, Sara Huggins.

Shelly and Emma would particularly like to thank all those who have taken part in management skills training courses with Common Threads or A Pair of Trainers. There are too many people to mention by name, but thanks to everybody for your enthusiasm and your honesty, and for letting us learn with you.

We would also like to thank family and friends for their enthusiasm and patience.

Glossary

Assertiveness	expressing your needs, wants, opinions, feelings in a direct, honest and appropriate way so as not to violate another person's rights
Awarding bodies	organisations that offer nationally recognised qualifications through study centres and colleges and monitor quality through a variety of systems such as external verifiers and moderators
Child-centred setting	an environment that is welcoming to children, gives them a free choice of activities, and values their opinions and views
Children	in this book, anyone aged 0–16 years
Disability	a restriction on the way a person can live day to day in current society due to lack of services and facilities
Feedback	giving another person or group of people verbal or written communication on their practice
Good practice	an acceptable and recognised way of working which is effective and fair to all, such as implementing anti-discriminatory policies
Harassment	direct or indirect discrimination through a verbal or physical attack that offends a person or makes them feel that their rights have been denied or abused
Homophobia	prejudice against gay men and lesbians because of their sexual preferences
Impairment	the inability to do something such as hear fully, or walk without the aid of a stick
Inclusive practice	see definition in Chapter 7 (p. 64)
Manager	the person responsible for the setting, who could sometimes be the deputy manager, a supervisor, a senior worker or a coordinator
Oppression	giving a person or a group of people a low status because of prejudice and stereotyping
Policies and procedures	written documentation on how the setting operates and how it meets the legal requirements
Practice	how a person carries out their work
Practitioner	a person working or volunteering in the setting who has training and experience
Prejudice	a fixed attitude based on prejudged ideas or information about a person, group or community; normally understood as being a negative approach and often influenced by societal judgements of the time

Principles and values	guidelines that underpin the work of the Early Years and Playwork sector, as agreed at the time by practitioners
Racism	treating a person or group of people as less than equal because of their race. The Race Relations Act defines race as colour, nationality, ethnic or national origins. The Children Act 1989 adds culture and religion and language.
Reflective practice	see definition in Chapter 3 (p. 21)
Settings	services such as after-school clubs, adventure playgrounds, playgroups, nurseries, open-access schemes, holiday playschemes, crèches, and out-of-school playwork schemes
Sexism	stereotyping an individual or discriminating against them because of their gender, which is believed to give them certain traits and certain roles in society
Sexual orientation	how an individual chooses their sexuality in society
Special Needs	requirements of children whose developmental stage does not accord with the general level of development either because of a physical condition or learning difficulties or emotional and behavioural difficulties, or because they are gifted
Stereotyping	a method of labelling people based on assumptions gained through socialisation, prejudices and preconceived ideas. Stereotyping is bound up with expectations of roles played in society and norms placed on those roles.
Tokenism	an action or remark that attempts to show good practice but which is not genuine

Introduction

People who work in child-centred settings are generally thought of as part of the 'caring profession'. The long-held values of respect, empowerment, equality of opportunity, individual attention and so on have ensured that children have indeed been well cared for in the vast majority of settings. With increased government regulation and intervention, practitioners are required to raise standards of provision even further and also demonstrate clearly the value of the care that they provide to individual children. 'Care' is therefore embedded in the practice base of those who work in child-centred settings.

Not so well established is the concept of belonging to a 'profession'. Working with children, caring for them (in either a formal or an informal sense) has been regarded as non-professional, low-paid work. Many women have even described their role as a 'vocation'. Love of children, time and patience have historically been seen as key indicators of the ability to work with children. Despite often needing to work in their own time and receiving very little support or training, those caring for children are believed to have reward enough from the role itself.

Yet with current levels of government support and regulation come further demands on our time, our energy and our skills. 'Caring' is no longer enough to justify funding, wages, training opportunities, career paths, status and recognition. Government ministers have issued challenges (*Playwords* July 1998) to the field to act as professionals, to prove why we ought to be taken seriously as a valuable part of the workforce of this country. Having risen to these challenges to some extent, the field is seeing rewards for its efforts, with more people choosing to work with children as a career. There is also emerging in society an increasing understanding of the importance and value of working with children. In other words, a revolution is taking place – a battle for professional status in a workforce for whom the caring comes naturally, but belonging to a profession does not.

And who then shall lead this revolution? It is the managers of the nurseries, the after-school clubs, the adventure playgrounds, the children's homes, the family centres, the playbuses who find themselves inadvertently on the front line. In the past, managers/supervisors/leaders/senior practitioners in child-centred settings have been the people with whom the buck stopped, who took the awkward decisions, dealt with the paperwork and went home at the end of the day having kept the place ticking over. Valuable though this role may have been in the past, these skills will not suffice to lead the revolution of professionalisation and to enable the field to complete its journey from undervalued carers to highly skilled and valued professionals.

Nowadays managers in child-centred settings need to be able to draw on a whole new set of skills to help them to promote professional attitudes and behaviour throughout their settings. Often highly skilled senior practitioners themselves, promoted because of their experience and commitment, managers in child-centred settings have to be able to effect a culture shift within their organisation, employing an approach and a set of skills that usually have to be learnt on the job. It is relatively easy to learn new skills which will help you to deal with the routine tasks of management in a child-centred setting (how to undertake risk assessments, run a bookings system, organise a large-scale event, write reports and so on). Yet how do managers get others to improve their practice, develop their skills, meet new standards, improve the service – all of which are nowadays fundamental requirements of being included in the ranks of the professionals?

This book seeks to help managers in child-centred settings to **be** managers. 'Doing' management (filling in the forms, organising the money, developing the policies) is an important part of the role of a manager in a child-centred setting, and there is now an increasing amount of training and support available for this. Yet very little support exists for what could be seen to be an even more vital part of the role – that of being a leader. If managers are leading the professional revolution, they also have to be seen to be professionals in their role. To be able to role-model professionalism, they have to be able to be professional in their outlook and their approach. This means being able to lead a team of people in order to provide the best possible service for the children in their setting. It may sound like an easy task, but it requires skills which do not come naturally to many people – being able to influence, motivate and guide others, or, in other words, leadership skills.

In this book we will be using both management and leadership theories and techniques, and we will also sometimes use the terms 'manager' and 'leader' interchangeably. However, we should make it clear that 'management' and 'leadership' do not in fact mean the same thing. Ideally, every manager should also be a leader. However, it is possible to be a manager without having or using any leadership skills at all. The following definition by Hersey (1984) helps to clarify the difference: '**Management is working with and through others to accomplish organisational goals. Leadership is any attempt to influence the behaviour of another individual or group.**'

In other words, in an ideal world we would all work together in our groups with a manager whose sole job it would be to monitor our progress against what we were trying to achieve and praise us once we had achieved it! However, we know that life is never really that straightforward, and that we all need motivation, direction, instruction, support, encouragement, development and so on to change and improve the way we do things. So an effective manager, one who is really working to accomplish organisational goals, also needs to be able to influence the way their team does things – and for this they need leadership skills. We have identified what we consider to be the ten most important leadership skills for the ten chapters of this book. There are of course many other leadership skills that managers of child-centred settings need, and we have broken down each of the ten skills to include some of those other skills.

What do we mean by 'manager in a child-centred setting'?

No child-centred setting is the same as another, and even those which are called by the same title (e.g. playcentres, nurseries) have very different structures within which staff are employed. Managers may be

- counted within adult–children ratios, or supernumerary

- in charge of more than one setting

- managing teams of 2–200+

- working in an office space

- doing paperwork at home

- chairing a voluntary management committee

- working with or without deputies

- paid or unpaid.

We have endeavoured to reflect as many different types of setting in which people work with children throughout the book as possible, although we will not of course have come anywhere near including them all. Similarly, we have tried to make both the theory and the practical information applicable to anybody who is in a management or leadership role within a child-centred setting.

Whatever the context, and whatever the job title, the basic role of a manager in a child-centred setting can be stated quite simply as follows: **A manager in a child-centred setting is the person responsible for making sure that the aim of the setting is achieved.** Again, this appears to be a relatively simple task on the surface, but requires a set of skills not normally associated with caring for children. This book aims to help managers of child-centred settings to fill that gap.

We would welcome comment and feedback on the book – please send your thoughts to info@commonthreads.co.uk or contact us via the publishers.

CHAPTER 1

Confidence

Some readers may be surprised to find confidence the first skill that is covered by this book. In the introduction we gave a definition of the role of the manager of a child-centred setting, and explained that managers need to be able to use leadership skills in order to influence others so that they will achieve the organisational goals. Any attempt to help others to change their behaviour requires confidence on the part of the manager.

Essential skills for developing confidence

- Vision

- Self-esteem

- Assertiveness

- Long-term thinking

- Accepting compliments

- Staying in the present

- Accepting imperfection

- Sharing responsibility

- Being accountable

Why is confidence important for managers of child-centred settings?

There are two types of confidence that managers need when working in child-centred settings:

1 confidence in the fact that it is indeed part of their role to influence the behaviour of others so that the setting works towards its organisational aim and achieves the best possible quality of service for the children who go there

2 confidence in their own abilities to manage and lead others in the way that will help them to achieve their organisational aim.

It is important for managers, and those with whom they work, to understand that the role of the manager should be a *pro-active* role, not a *re-active* one. Very often managers in child-centred settings are seen as the people with whom the buck stops. While it is, of course, true to say that taking ultimate responsibility is part of your role, a manager is not simply a trouble-shooter or an administrator. A manager also needs to be 'out there', taking a lead in shaping the sort of service the setting is delivering to the children you work with, and making sure that you are meeting all the expectations about how good your service should be. Chapter 2 looks at this area of a manager's role in more detail.

Not everybody understands this as a vital part of the role of a manager. Managers can often find themselves in situations where their own managers do not fulfil this role. Not only then do they not have a good role model to follow, but they also have to have enough confidence to be able to reshape their role and to be accountable for that to their superiors. In some situations individual team members (or even whole teams) can find it difficult to accept their manager as somebody who will be focused on developing the setting and inevitably making changes to the way that people work. So managers in child-centred settings need a double dose of confidence: confidence in their own abilities to be able to be pro-active in their setting and to develop and shape the ways things are done, and enough confidence in their role to be able to explain to others that this is what their job is about.

Exuding confidence is not an option when we manage child-centred settings. No confidence, no leadership – and no leadership, no vision. The children you work with deserve the very best service you and your team can give them – and it's up to you to make sure that they get it. It is not possible to do it all yourself, and therefore you need to be able to manage others in a way that encourages them to do it with you – in other words, you need to be confident enough to be a leader.

Other chapters in this book will help you with specific skills, such as decision-making, time management and giving feedback. But before you can acquire such skills, you need the confidence to believe that your role is about shaping, influencing and guiding, and that you have the ability to be able to achieve this.

So the person to start with is **you** and how you feel about your role right now.

Developing your own skills

Self-esteem

All of us need it, very few of us have enough of it. Good self-esteem is vital in being able to feel confident about your role as a manager, the decisions you make at work, and your ability to deal with awkward situations and difficult people. If you get out of bed in the morning thinking that you are a capable and competent person, looking forward confidently to the challenges that the day will bring, then congratulations! Your self-esteem is probably just about right. However, if you go to work worrying about that conversation you're going to have to have, the paperwork you dread completing or the telephone call you've been putting off making, then maybe you don't feel good about your abilities to manage such situations satisfactorily and your self-esteem could do with a bit of a boost.

Low self-esteem can be due to the gap between what you perceive to be your ideal characteristics and what you feel the reality actually is. For example, you may feel that it is really important in life to be patient with others, but in reality you know that you have a bit of a short fuse. Many people spend their lives striving to fill this gap, rather than accepting that the gap exists. In doing so, they are focusing on something they perceive to be negative about themselves. The likelihood is that they will not be able to close the gap to their liking, and will therefore feel dissatisfied with themselves – or, in other words, suffer from low self-esteem.

This does not mean, of course, that most of us could not try to be a bit more patient, a bit more creative, a bit better with paperwork – whatever we would rather we were. But the key to good self-esteem is to be able to notice the gap and to manage it, rather than trying to fill it, which inevitably leads to those feelings of being out of control and powerless. So instead of telling ourselves, 'I'm really bad at making decisions, and I must be more decisive', we need to treat ourselves a bit more gently. 'I'm not very confident about making decisions, and I would like to be, so I will do a few things to help me to develop more skills in decision-making' is an approach that will help us to increase the skills gradually and build self-esteem rather than destroy it.

To have good self-esteem means feeling competent and capable in yourself – that you have the skills and abilities to cope with whatever comes your way. It is important to notice that, in the vast majority of tricky situations, there is nobody telling you that you can't cope – except you. Dealing with difficult conversations with parents, for example, may not come easily to many of us, but people with good self-esteem will not dread these types of situation or put them off, because they know that they can handle them, however difficult it might be. Good self-esteem gives us confidence even when we may not feel confident, because whatever the situation, we will still feel at ease with ourselves afterwards.

Assertiveness

It's one of those chicken-and-egg situations, isn't it? – the more confidence we have, the more assertive we can be, and the more assertive we are, the more confident we feel!

It's important to remember that assertiveness is not the same as being aggressive. Some people seem to confuse an authoritarian style of behaviour with assertive behaviour, and the two are actually not the same at all. It is in fact more helpful to think of assertive behaviour as being 'quietly confident'. To put it another way, assertiveness is 'behaviour which helps us to communicate clearly and confidently our needs, wants and feelings to other people without in any way abusing their human rights' (Lindenfield 1986). This may sound reasonably simple and straightforward, but there are several ways in which we contrive not to make our wants, needs and feelings known, such as:

- Using 'you' instead of 'I' in order to avoid taking responsibility for what we really think or feel. For example, 'You can tell that she's fed up because . . .' instead of 'I think she's fed up because . . .'

- Using phrases such as 'I wonder if' and 'Would you mind' instead of making a direct request of a colleague.

- Saying 'we' when we really mean 'you'! For example, 'Could we try to keep the craft cupboard tidier so that we can find things?' instead of 'I would like you to keep the craft cupboard tidier so that you can find what you need.'

- Using other people's perceived or imagined feelings and thoughts in a way that suggests that it is what everybody else thinks or feels instead of what you think or feel. For example, 'The rest of the team wants you to . . .' instead of 'I would prefer you to . . .'

It is very important for managers to be able to take responsibility for their own wants and feelings and to communicate those to others. Apart from ensuring that those wants and feelings are clearly communicated and unambiguous, such assertive behaviour also sets a good role model to follow and encourages others to adopt assertive behaviour patterns. If you recognise any of the non-assertive phrases above as those which you would normally use, try to gradually introduce the phrases which start with 'I' instead. This may feel strange at first, but you should notice the difference in how much more confident using such phrases makes you sound and feel after a while.

Gael Lindenfield (1986) gives the following steps to take in order to behave assertively:

- Decide what you want

- Decide if it is fair

- Ask clearly for it

- Do not be afraid of taking risks

- Be calm and relaxed

- Express your feelings openly

- Give and take compliments easily

- Give and take fair criticism.

Many of us would like to think that this is how we behave all the time, and some people do indeed behave assertively without having to think about it. However, it is quite a difficult skill to master. How many of us, for example, like to think that we take fair criticism, whereas in fact we are apt to become defensive and try to explain ourselves when somebody tells us about something we could do differently? Like any other skill, assertiveness is something many of us need to practise and continue to develop throughout our lives.

Long-term thinking

If you think your confidence does need a bit of a boost at the moment, it's not reasonable to expect that to happen overnight. Developing confidence takes a combination of experience, skills, knowledge and time. There are some publications listed in the Bibliography at the end of this book that may help you to develop confidence in the longer term.

In the meantime, however, there's no reason why you can't appear more confident than you actually feel, and see if this makes a difference to how you feel and how other people feel about you. Here are some techniques to give your confidence a short-term boost – and, practised over a period of time, these can also help confidence to develop in the long term:

- *Smile*

  Yes, it's that easy – smiling really does make us feel better. It has another bonus, which is that it also makes other people feel better too! Smiling is a very useful technique when thinking about that self-esteem gap – it is quite difficult to feel nervous or worried about doing something if you are smiling. Try to remember to smile before the start of any conversation – positive or negative. The news may be bad, but the delivery doesn't have to be!

- *Walk like the manager, talk like a leader*

  Can people tell who the person with ultimate responsibility is in your setting? Not because you are the person bossing people around or with the loudest voice in the place, but because you are the person who exudes confidence and inspires confidence in others around you. Develop that feeling of 'quiet confidence' – of being in control of yourself and of whatever situation comes your way – and others will assume that you are in control too.

- *See difficult situations as a series of stepping stones*

  Many people see difficult situations as a set of barriers or hurdles. If you change the way you approach such situations by envisaging a set of steps to help you to sort it out, you will feel your confidence levels rising as you take each step.

- *Tackle first the things in your daily routine that knock your confidence*

  If you go into work dreading the difficult conversation you need to have, or coming up with ways of avoiding writing the report that you can't get your head round, make a decision that you will do that thing first (and stick to this decision!). By doing so you will probably find that it actually wasn't as difficult as you thought it was going to be, and you will get an instant confidence boost for the rest of the day.

Accepting compliments

Our confidence increases when we feel good about ourselves. We can help ourselves to feel good about ourselves by taking positive steps to increase our self-esteem. We can also allow others to further enhance our confidence by accepting compliments that other people pay us. For some reason, however, many of us find this really difficult, and so we start saying things such as, 'Oh, I don't really listen well/give positive feedback/understand the accounts', apparently in order to deny that the compliment is true. The other common response is to make a joke out of the compliment: 'Well, you've just caught me on a good day – you should have seen me in a mess with this yesterday!'

When somebody says something nice about something you've done, or a quality that you have, it is vital for your confidence levels to accept it gracefully. This means doing two things. First of all, say nothing but 'thank you'. Don't be tempted to enter into the 'Oh, it was nothing' routine – somebody wants to pay you a compliment, so let them! The second thing you must do is to give yourself some credit. They really did want to acknowledge something that they have noticed that they like about you – it is very unlikely that they made up the compliment. Believe that you have done a good thing and give yourself a pat on the back.

Staying in the present

Focus on what is going on at the present time. Don't worry about what might happen as a result of what you are saying and doing – put your energy into concentrating on what's happening in the here and now. The present is the only time you can do anything about. If you worry about what could happen, your confidence levels will drop as you waste energy agonising about things that could go wrong but may never actually take place.

Accepting imperfection

Earlier we talked about the need to accept that we are not perfect as a way of developing our self-esteem. Very few people can be good at everything. We need to be able to accept that we are not perfect people in order to feel confident about ourselves.

Another important area in which to accept imperfection is that everybody makes mistakes. In our working lives we will make, as will become clear with hindsight, wrong decisions, we will misjudge situations, we will do things that we really could have done better. By and large, most of the things that we could have done differently will not be major disasters. We need to aim for 'good enough' outcomes to our actions, and to be pleased when this happens, rather than aiming for perfection and our confidence levels dropping when we inevitably fail. Managers need to accept their own mistakes and use them to help develop their professional practice. Chapter 3 looks at ways of doing this. The key to maintaining confidence levels while learning from our mistakes is to approach professional mistakes professionally, rather than to see them as personal failures.

Managers have to learn to accept imperfection in others as well as in themselves. We have talked so far in this book about the need for managers to act as leaders, which involves affecting the way that other people behave. It is perfectly acceptable to expect to be able to support people in making changes to their working practices, in order to improve the service being offered in line with your organisational objectives. However, it is not realistic to expect that you will change the way that people think and act. Individuals can only change their own practice, and it is important to realise that nobody else can do it for them. Managers can request, encourage and support change in individuals, but they cannot expect it. Managers cannot hope to change people by the force of their will or their support, but must instead rely on people to make changes for themselves. This can, of course, lead to a situation where there is not enough change in an individual for practice to improve, and it will then be up to the manager to decide what level of imperfection can reasonably be accommodated in the setting. The important skill here is accepting that not everybody will get everything right all of the time, and once we work from that basis it is much easier to be confident about what we are expecting to achieve.

Sharing responsibility

Managers are, of course, ultimately responsible for what goes on in their setting. However, within this overall responsibility, there are many things that managers can support others in being responsible for. Managers in child-centred settings sometimes tend to take on too much responsibility – responsibility for how others feel, how other people behave, for example. This is not to say, of course, that managers do not need to notice and to respond to other people's behaviour and feelings, but responding appropriately is different from taking responsibility for those things. It can also be the case that managers sometimes take inappropriate responsibility for parts of other people's jobs – managers in child-centred settings are martyrs to the maxim, 'if you want a job done properly, do it yourself'. They can often fill their day with things that other people haven't done, on the basis that it is quicker to do it themselves than remind the person who should be doing it to get on with it. Not only does this mean that the manager cannot perform their own role of developing the service, but also it quite often means that they suffer from a lack of confidence, as they feel powerlessness in 'having' to cope with everything. Managers who develop the skill of sharing responsibility see their confidence increase as they realise that they are capable of effecting change in their setting.

Being accountable

We use the phrase 'professional integrity' later in the book, and by this we mean accepting responsibility and accountability. It is very easy to blame things on others and to avoid looking honestly at our own part in situations that could have gone better. Confident managers do not seek to avoid being held to account, and this acceptance of responsibility increases their confidence levels. This is because others respect them, and they also respect themselves, for being able to deal with the responsibility.

Putting it into practice

- Develop confidence in your role as somebody who should be leading and developing the work of your team.

- Improve your self-esteem to increase your confidence.

- Accept imperfection in yourself and others.

- Try to notice when your behaviour could be more assertive and practise assertiveness skills.

- Accept compliments from others with a smile instead of an excuse!

- Decide what your boundaries are and what other people need to take responsibility for.

- Accept that increasing confidence levels takes time and practice to achieve.

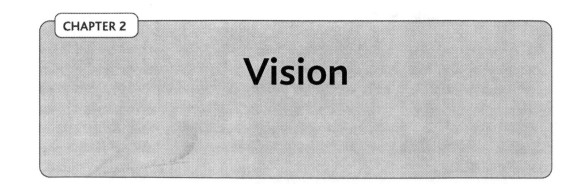

CHAPTER 2

Vision

As people who work with children, we are incredibly lucky. Wherever we work, our jobs involve helping children to develop skills, knowledge and values. This may involve different things, depending on the setting – some may excel in social development, others in educational development, others in physical well-being. Whatever the focus, all settings should contribute to the present and future well-being of children.

When asked, many managers are able to describe how their setting plays an important part in individual children's development. However, this important part of child-centred settings is often taken for granted on a day-to-day basis. Settings rarely set out their vision for the children who go there, but instead tend to use bland descriptions of their services that can sound like the descriptions of similar settings across the land. This is unfortunate, as not only do these descriptions play down what the settings are achieving for children, but also they hinder the management of the setting.

Essential skills for developing vision

- Confidence
- Drive
- Describing vision
- Setting clear aims and objectives
- Communicating vision

Why is vision important?

Vision can be described as the ability to think about the future in an imaginative and creative way. In the context of working with children, vision is important to help us to do two things:

1   to predict the benefits our work can offer to children in the short, medium and long term

2   to describe the sort of goals the setting should work towards and what further opportunities it could offer to children, staff, volunteers, the community, etc.

Vision is therefore vital in knowing why your setting exists and where it is heading. This may sound obvious, but it is very difficult to start or continue any journey unless you know where you are going to. Settings that do not have any sort of vision to work towards are in danger of getting stale, and therefore not delivering the best possible service for the children. Managers need to be able to hold and develop a vision so that the rest of the team are constantly aware of what their work is about and why it is important to change and develop their practice. Having vision improves the service the setting delivers for children, as well as keeping individual team members focused and motivated.

Managers in child-centred settings can sometimes feel that they are on some sort of never-ending treadmill – work life appears to be a perpetual cycle of planning, paperwork and problems. The 'doing' and the 'fun' of working with children can sometimes seem very remote. It is all too easy to get bogged down in the daily grind of administration, regulations and meetings and to lose touch with the reasons for working in this field in the first place.

One of the reasons that managers lose touch with the value of their work is because they cannot connect the day-to-day 'managing' of paper and people with the long-term benefits of the direct work with the children. They forget that, while they may not be providing input into the welfare and development of individual children all day, every day, their role is just as crucial in their setting as that of anybody who does face-to-face work. It is the manager's role to ensure that their whole setting is achieving the very best it can for the children who attend, and it is only the manager who can influence this in any meaningful, sustainable way. While inspectors, development workers, trainers and others may help settings periodically, they cannot ensure that that setting is constantly monitoring and improving the way it delivers benefits for children. Only the manager, working regularly and consistently with their team, can make sure that children get the best service possible. When seen in this light, the role of the manager is transformed from the person with the shovel and the bucket to the person who ensures that the setting is making a difference to children's lives.

Vision is important, then, because it is closely tied in with motivation. If people generally know why they are doing something, and they can see the value in what they are doing, it is more likely they will perform better in order to achieve the task. It is much easier to be motivated by the fact that you are ensuring the future of the group by doing the funding application to a tight deadline than it is to be motivated by the threat of your boss being cross with you if you miss that deadline. In day-to-day practice terms, it is possible to motivate people on even the most routine tasks if they can see the benefit to the children. Keeping the equipment cupboard tidy might be a tedious chore, but even this can be described in terms of the benefits that children will gain from a tidier cupboard. Of course, being motivated by vision doesn't work for everybody – we have to recognise that some team members are motivated by other things that have more to do with reward and personal achievement. However, being able to describe the value of an individual's work in terms of benefits for the children does help people to understand the importance of daily routines and the part that they play in helping children to develop.

Personal and organisational vision

It is important to acknowledge that there can be two types of vision in a child-centred setting – personal vision and organisational vision. In an ideal world, the personal vision of the manager is reflected in the organisational vision of the setting, and vice versa. However, there can be situations where the vision of the manager is different from that of the organisation for which they work.

For example, a manager who goes into playwork to pursue their vision about the value of free play for children could find themselves managing childcare provision. Both open-access play provision and playcare settings have much to offer children and families, but they exist for different reasons and will therefore work towards different organisational goals.

Such a conflict can cause great difficulties, both for the individual concerned and for the organisation. Managers can suffer from stress as a result of their vision being in conflict with that of their organisation. Organisations can suffer from a manager who is managing towards a personal vision, rather than an organisational one, as the organisation tries to go in one direction while the manager tries to go in another.

Sometimes managers need to accept such clashes of vision and work out strategies to help them to manage in spite of the conflict. At other times, it is fairer to everybody concerned for the manager to find another post where the values and vision of the organisation tie in more closely with their own.

Developing your own skills

Drive

Managers need to bring another 'p' into their daily working lives, to counteract the planning, paperwork, and problems. That fourth 'p' is **passion**. Like any other job, working in child-centred settings can be enormously tiring and frustrating. But it can also be enormously rewarding and satisfying, with dozens of opportunities in a day to make a positive impact on a child's development.

There are, of course, some people working in child-centred settings who do not feel passionate about their work. Managers therefore need drive – or, in other words, the determination and ambition to ensure that vision is carried through the entire setting. Passion is the foundation for drive, because if you are passionate about something, you will do your utmost to make it happen. The following questions can help you to think about what you are passionate about in your work:

- What do I most look forward to in my working day?

- What makes me smile at work?

- When I go home, what makes me happy to have been at work today?

- What positive thing do I most want to achieve during my working week?

Remember that when answering the last question, you need to identify something positive, rather than simply describing something that you want to stop happening! For example, there is a huge difference between wanting to help the team to work together more effectively and hoping that nobody falls out with anyone this week.

Describing vision

In the introduction to this book, we defined management as 'working with and through others to accomplish organisational goals' (Hersey 1984). This definition, of course, prompts the question: what are organisational goals?

Different child-centred settings will have different reasons for existing. These may include

- helping children with educational achievement

- enabling children to take part in a wide range of play opportunities

- developing children's social skills and self-esteem

- helping parents with parenting skills

- community development objectives, such as crime prevention.

Whatever the motive for existing, each setting will have something unique to offer to children and their families. This intention, of offering some sort of service or support to children and/or families, is what we mean by an organisational goal.

Organisational goals in child-centred settings should be visionary – that is, they should describe what the setting hopes to achieve for the people who use it, rather than just describing the type of environment that they provide, or what you think you are already doing. It is important to remember that even when child-centred settings are set up to make a profit, the vision for the children can and should still be described.

There are many terms used to describe what a setting does and why it does it. The above definition uses the term 'organisational goals' and you will probably also be familiar with phrases such as mission statements, aims and objectives, operational plans, etc. We will concentrate on expressing this description as a set of aims and objectives, as being able to develop clear aims and objectives is a very useful skill that can be used in many different areas of management. The term 'organisational aim' therefore refers to the description of what your setting hopes to achieve by its work.

Setting clear aims and objectives

The place to start with aims and objectives is to understand the difference between the two. This difference can be defined as follows:

An **aim** sets out what you are hoping to achieve, and therefore aims always start with the word '*to*'.

Objectives spell out the way you are going to achieve your aim, and they therefore always start with '*by*'. Objectives are like the stepping-stones you need to follow to achieve your aim.

Another general rule to abide by is that you only need one aim but each aim can have as many objectives as you need. Of course, as with all 'general rules' there are exceptions, and we will look at some of the exceptions to this general rule in other chapters.

Once you have got your aim and objectives for your setting drafted out, you need to find out whether they are going to be useful to you as a manager; that is, whether you will be able to use them to lead and monitor the work of your setting. You can use a handy acronym to find out how useful they are – SMART, which stands for specific, measurable, achievable, relevant, and timed. Checking to see whether your aim and your objectives are SMART will help you to make sure that they are useful to you in managing your setting. You should also find that your aim and objectives automatically become more visionary as they become clearer, more specific and measurable.

Specific

You need to look at your aim and see whether it says exactly what it means – or is it a bit vague and woolly? For example, many child-centred settings have words like 'safe', 'happy', and 'secure' in their aim. Are these specific enough to help you to manage your setting – in other words, can you actually say what 'safety' means in the context of, for example, an after-school club which caters for 4–12-year-olds? After all, what's safe in one set of circumstances will not be safe in others (and vice versa) – therefore can a word like 'safety' be used to describe accurately what a child-centred setting aims to achieve? And likewise with 'happy' – if some children are sad in a nursery, does this mean that the manager's job is to go round cheering everybody up in order to achieve the aim of the setting?

Measurable

Will you be able to tell when you are getting close to achieving your aim and when it has been achieved? For example, in the case of words such as 'safe' and 'happy', will you be able to measure these? It is, in fact, very difficult to measure an aim or part of an aim that is not specific. If your aim cannot be measured, then it is not going to help you to manage your setting – because if you can't tell if you're achieving your aim, then you might as well not have one! When thinking about whether an aim is measurable or not, we also need to think about the methods which will be used to measure it.

Achievable

If an aim isn't measurable, then it won't be achievable, as it will be impossible to tell when it has been achieved. Both aims and objectives need to be achievable – maybe not now, or in a few weeks, but in the future – however long you decide that will be. We can ask certain questions to check whether it is achievable; for example, do we have (or can we get) enough resources to do it? Do we have enough time to finish it? Do we have enough expertise to achieve what we want to achieve? It is important to be realistic when thinking about what is achievable – while working towards a vision is helpful in developing the service, it is not helpful to set your sights so high that you will never get anywhere near achieving it.

Relevant

Aims and objectives need to be relevant to your setting, rather than to any setting. You need to ensure that your organisational aim is related to your environment, your funding, your community, your reason for existing – whatever it is that makes your project unique.

Timed

Aims and objectives should normally state when you are aiming to have them achieved by – this gives you a date or a time to aim for and to check against to see if you are on track. However, in the case of an organisational aim, it would only be useful to put a time limit on the aim or the objectives if your setting operates on a short-term or time-limited basis (for example, a summer holiday playscheme or a one-year funded parent and toddler group). In this way your organisational aim can include your long-term vision for the future.

CASE STUDY

Jo, the manager at Dun'playin Playcentre, decided to revisit their organisational aim and objectives. She couldn't really remember what the aim and objectives were, so she went to dig them out of a file. They read as follows:

> The playworkers of Dun'playin Playcentre are committed to providing an environment which meets the needs of all children. Our overriding aim is to create a safe and caring environment where every child can enjoy themselves in a happy, friendly atmosphere.

Jo settled down with the SMART checklist to take a long, hard and honest look at whether this aim helped her to manage the playcentre.

The first thing that she noticed was that there was nothing in the aim about play. 'Odd, that, given that we're a playcentre', she thought, and made a note. She also looked at the phrase about meeting the needs of all children. 'Is that really achievable?' she wondered – 'and even if it were, it doesn't say what needs we want to meet.' Jo pondered for a while about the word 'caring' – after all, what's 'caring' on the part of a parent is different from the way that playworkers care for children. 'Maybe that isn't specific enough – just like "safe" is rather vague. After all, we've got a twelve-foot climbing tower in the yard – that couldn't really be described as 100 per cent safe but the kids get so much out of it we certainly wouldn't want to take it down.' She also looked at the idea in the aim of children enjoying themselves, and realised that they didn't always actually want to enjoy themselves. 'Sometimes they come here to let off steam, sometimes they want to moan about their teachers or their parents, sometimes they just want to sit and do nothing and then go home again – and all of that's OK, although I wouldn't class any of that as "enjoying themselves" particularly', she thought.

Jo's SMART checklist looked like this:

Specific – caring, safe, happy, friendly can all be interpreted in different ways and therefore are not specific enough. Play isn't mentioned and should be.

Measurable – you can't measure whether we are meeting the needs of all children! Safe, caring, etc. are also not measurable.

Achievable – meeting the needs of all children is not really possible. Also not every child wants to enjoy themselves, therefore that part is not achievable.

Relevant – our 'overriding' aim is actually to help children to play, so not very relevant to us as it stands.

Timed – this one doesn't apply as we operate all year and are part of a funded local authority service (hopefully!).

Once she had finished her SMART checklist, Jo realised that she would either have to manage the playcentre in a very different way in order to meet this aim, or she would have to rewrite the aim in order to reflect exactly what the playcentre was there to do. She could see from the exercise that the existing aim did not help her to manage the centre, and that if she did try to use it then it would actually get in the way of the work that the centre was trying to achieve. Jo therefore decided to rewrite the organisational aim, trying to make it SMART as she went, and this is what she came up with:

'Dun'playin Playcentre aims to meet the play needs of all children.'

'Well, it's certainly short and sweet', thought Jo, 'but is it SMART?'

S – it is specific as far as it goes, but it doesn't say which children, so it could be more specific.

M – it is measurable, because we can assess play needs using some of the play theory.

A – it is achievable, but we need to say how we can achieve it in our objectives.

R – it is relevant, because it describes what we focus on here.

T – it doesn't need to be timed, but some of the objectives might need to be.

Jo then tweaked the aim in the light of this SMART exercise and added the objectives, which she also made SMART. By the time she'd finished, the aim and objectives read like this:

Aim

Dun'playin Playcentre aims to meet the play needs of all children between the ages of 5 and 15 years from the Downs Estate.

Objectives

We will do this by

- identifying the play needs of individual children within three weeks of them joining the playcentre
- responding to these play needs by ensuring that appropriate play types and materials are available at all times
- continuously assessing the play needs of the children and meeting differing needs as they occur
- providing support to individual children when required
- providing support to groups of children when required
- ensuring that fees are kept at a minimum to enable full access.

When she had finished, Jo decided that managing the playcentre according to this set of aims and objectives was going to be a lot easier. Now she could see what she was supposed to be managing, and, just as importantly, her team would be able to see clearly what they were supposed to be doing. 'To be fair,' Jo reflected, 'we are doing quite a lot of this anyway, but perhaps not in such a structured way as we could do. We'll need to work out the details now – how we assess and record play needs, for example. Perhaps I could turn each objective into another set of aims and objectives – that would help me work out how to achieve each one.'

Jo could see that her objectives should all add up to show how the aim was going to be achieved and, in the same way, each objective could be turned into an aim by itself with its own set of objectives to show how the staff team could achieve it. In this way, the team would all have a shared vision of what their jobs were achieving for children, which they hadn't really had before.

Communicating vision

Once the organisational aim is clear and SMART, it is important not to put it back in the file and forget about it. A set of organisational aims and objectives are incredibly useful management tools – not only for managers themselves, but also so that team members understand how the setting should operate. An organisational aim should therefore be a living document, which is used and reviewed as a part of everyday practice. Here are just some of the ways in which you can communicate your organisational aim:

- Use it when evaluating pieces of work or the work of your whole setting.

- Make sure that you make reference to it in team meetings, committee meetings, etc.

- Remind yourself of what the aim of the setting is each week.

- Put it on the wall / notice boards.

- Include it in all leaflets and publicity.

- Make sure that every policy clearly states the aim and says how you will achieve it.

- Ask the children if they think that the aim is being achieved.

Putting it into practice

- If you're not already sure, find out what the vision for your setting is.

- Try to describe this vision in terms of benefit for the children as accurately as possible.

- Make sure that your organisational aim reflects the vision of the setting.

- Use SMART to ensure that your organisational aim will help you to manage your setting according to the vision.

- Use every opportunity to communicate the organisational aim to others, both inside and outside your organisation.

- Be prepared to adapt or change the organisational aim if and when it no longer reflects the up-to-date vision for your setting.

CHAPTER 3

Reflective practice

Managers in child-centred settings may already be familiar with the term 'reflective practice' in the context of face-to-face work with children. It has been used to describe an approach where practitioners 'step back sometimes from what seems "normal" or "obvious" to us in children's play, learning and development' (Lindon 2001).

There are many different ways of using and describing reflective practice. It can generally be described as a tool for self-evaluation, in that it enables us to learn from our achievements and our mistakes by assessing our own practice. This chapter focuses on reflective practice as a technique which helps us to learn from our part in interactions with other people, as these interactions play such a large part in the role of a manager in a child-centred setting. Many other areas of work can be monitored and evaluated by using the techniques described later in this book. However, it is difficult to evaluate our interactions with others in the same way, as there are very few prescribed ways in which we can behave in order to achieve a certain outcome to an interaction. There are so many variables in human behaviour that trying to use methods normally used to evaluate situations where pre-determined models exist becomes meaningless. Reflective practice, however, can help us to evaluate our interactions with others in terms of

- What we do

- How we do it

- Why we do it that way

- Whether we should do it that way in the future.

Essential skills for developing reflective practice

- Confidence

- Staying in the present

- Accepting imperfection

- Honesty

- Flexibility

- Acknowledging personal success

- Professional integrity

- Analytical thinking

- Recognising barriers to reflective practice

Why is reflective practice important?

1 Reflective practice helps us to develop solutions to problems

Reflective practice stops us looking for answers where none exist. Managers are often keen to know 'how to deal with' the team member/parent/management committee member who is causing them strife. However, there are no 'templates' for the huge range of interactions which managers in child-centred settings deal with – there are only approaches and solutions. Interacting with different people at different times will produce different results. When you add into the equation that managers are people too, then we can see that any hope of 'getting it right' all the time is just not realistic.

Being a reflective practitioner means that we are able to start from a different point. Instead of saying, for example, 'I need to know how to stop children fighting', the reflective practitioner is able to draw on their experiences and their knowledge and ask, 'What have I learnt in other situations that might help me in situations where children fight?' Because, of course, there is no one way to 'stop children fighting' – there are only different approaches and interventions which face-to-face workers can try.

2 Reflective practice saves us time and energy

Using reflective practice gives shape and consistency to what can appear to be a set of separate experiences. It helps us to learn from these apparently unconnected experiences by giving us a means of drawing on the behaviours and the actions we have used in other circumstances. Reflective practice gives us a structure from which to develop what we have learnt so that we can use this knowledge again, rather than having to start from scratch every time.

Managers of child-centred settings who are reflective practitioners don't need to bang their heads against a brick wall until 'the answer' appears to questions such as 'How can I get Mrs Bloggs to turn up for work on time?' Reflective practitioners know that looking for 'the answer' is a waste of time and precious energy. They ask instead, 'What can I use from other similar circumstances that I could try with Mrs Bloggs to get her to come to work on time?' Rather than waiting for the answer to appear, managers who are reflective practitioners get on with the job of developing different approaches to the problem based on their previous knowledge and experience.

3 Reflective practice helps us to develop our own practice

By using reflective practice we can start to make connections between what we wanted to achieve from our interactions and the part we played. This means that we can develop our own practice from apparently small events in our working lives. This makes reflective practice a particularly useful learning tool for managers in child-centred settings, as they often do not get feedback from others on their own practice (see Chapter 5 for more on giving feedback). There are several ways that managers of child-centred settings could get further support for developing their own reflective practice. These include

- discussions with your own manager

- finding a colleague from a similar setting who has the same sort of responsibilities as you

- talking to a colleague from within the field but with a different job role; for example, a development worker

- setting up a group of like-minded managers in your area to meet on a regular basis

- joining a web-based discussion group.

4 Reflective practice is good practice

It is now considered good practice for everybody working in child-centred settings to make use of reflective practice as part of their professional development and the development of the setting in which they work. If managers want to encourage the effective use of reflective practice across their setting, one way to do this is to lead the team by doing it themselves.

5 Reflective practice helps us to check theory against practice

Using reflective practice can provide us with a useful 'reality check'. It helps us to ensure that we are acting in the way that we believe we are acting. The field of working with children is awash with jargon which purports to describe the way we work. Phrases such as 'child-centred' and 'quality care' are now part of accepted professional terminology. Yet we do need to ensure that we are actually putting the words into practice. By thinking about the way in which we behave when working with others, the way we talk to parents, the way we play with children, the way we act in team meetings etc., we can discover whether we really are working in the way that we intend and in the way the standards of our setting require us to work.

Specific and continuous reflective practice

It is useful to think about two types of reflective practice when working in child-centred settings. Firstly, reflective practice can be a one-off analysis of a particular interaction and we describe this as specific reflective practice. This type of reflective practice can be used on a daily basis to look at how specific interactions have taken place. It is also often used as a development tool on training courses to help participants to 'think about a time when' and to consider how they would now act in a similar situation in the light of new knowledge or skills gained on the course. Managers can use specific reflective practice in team meetings and supervision sessions as a technique to encourage others to think about their own behaviour in certain situations.

Secondly, the term reflective practice is also increasingly used to describe a way in which professionals who work with children are encouraged to behave all the time, rather than simply reflecting on isolated events. The phrase 'reflective practitioner' is often used to mean somebody who continuously uses reflection as a way of monitoring their own interaction with others – in other words, they are constantly aware of their thoughts and actions and the impact that these may have on others.

Managers who use continuous reflective practice develop something like a background 'soundtrack' that runs throughout their working day and provides a running commentary on what they are doing. While they are going from one room of the nursery to the other, they think to themselves, 'How have I just walked through that room? Did I smile? Did I take time to comment on good practice? Or did I just rush through and ask somebody briefly to keep the room a bit tidier?' In continuous reflective practice, it is possible for the analysis and the development to happen all at the same time. In the scenario above, for example, an experienced reflective practitioner would be able to analyse their actions and make the necessary changes while they are walking through the next room. This type of reflective practice is therefore referred to in this chapter as 'continuous reflective practice'.

CASE STUDY

Stuart loved his job as a manager of a playcentre. He was enthusiastic about helping the children to feel that the centre was for them, and spent a lot of time talking to the volunteers and staff who worked there about the importance of involving the children in the running of the setting.

At the beginning of December, Stuart decided that they would decorate the centre for Christmas. At the start of one of the sessions he brought in a large Christmas tree and the children got very excited. One girl asked Stuart where the Christmas tree was going to stand, and Stuart told her that he was going to put it in the corner of the room. After doing this, he got out some tree decorations, and organised the children to decorate the tree by giving out the decorations and telling them where to hang each one on the tree.

> Stuart could have used continuous reflective practice to be aware of his actions during the activity, or he could have undertaken a piece of specific reflective practice after the event. Using either type of reflective practice, hopefully he would have noticed that his intention (of helping children to feel that the centre was theirs) did not match up with the outcome of the activity.

Five-stage reflective practice model

In order for reflective practice to be a useful learning tool, it needs to be carried out in a structured way. Giving a shape to our reflection helps us to understand exactly what it is that we are learning. For example, it is very difficult to learn from an interaction by simply telling ourselves that it went well. We need to be able to identify why it went well and what we did that helped that particular situation. There are five stages in our reflective practice model: intention, experience, actions, outcome, and development. Both continuous and specific reflective practice need to include all five stages. Remember that, for continuous reflective practice, we will need to assess the situation as it is taking place. For specific reflective practice, the model should be applied after the event.

1 Intention

First of all we need to reflect on the original purpose of the interaction. What are we (or were we) aiming to achieve by our part in the interaction? In the case study above, Stuart was keen to help the children to feel that it was 'their' centre.

2 Experience

Then we need to reflect on what actually happened and gather together a factual account of what took place before, during and/or after the interaction. Stuart would have noted that he made the decisions about where the tree went and how it was decorated.

3 Actions

The next stage involves noticing our actions during the interaction – what we said, felt, thought, etc. We need to take care to notice what actually took place, not what we would have liked to happen. Stuart might have noticed that he was in a bit of a hurry during that session and that he had told the children what to do rather than taking the time to help the children to make the decisions for themselves.

4 Outcome

We then need to assess the outcome of the interaction. Did it achieve, or is it achieving, what was originally intended? Again, honesty is vital here. Stuart would have noted that the tree got put up, but the children probably wouldn't have felt very involved in the process.

5 Development

Finally, what can be learnt from our part in the interaction? If it is achieving or has achieved its intended outcome, how did we act in order to help this to happen? If the intended outcome wasn't achieved, what could we have done differently in order to change the outcome of the situation? Stuart could take more time next time to involve the children and talk to them differently, by asking questions instead of giving them directions.

Developing your own skills

Staying in the present

It is very difficult for people who are too stressed, tired, anxious, afraid, etc. to carry out reflective practice effectively. This is either because they simply do not have the energy to stay focused in the present moment, or because their mind is whirring away with many different things and they are just too distracted to notice what they are doing and how they are doing it. Managers of child-centred settings need to be able to focus on what they are saying and doing in the here and now.

Accepting imperfection

Perfectionists have a really hard time in life because they find it difficult to get to grips with the fact that they are not perfect and neither are people they work with. One of the assumptions that lie behind the process of reflective practice is that sometimes we do get interactions with others right and sometimes we don't. Mastering the skill of reflective practice relies not only on our understanding this assumption, but also on our accepting it and really taking it to heart. Making mistakes is part of the learning and development process – it is not a sign of personal weakness or failure.

Honesty

Generally speaking, people who work in child-centred settings like to think they're doing a good job. Effective reflective practice sometimes makes us notice that we haven't acted in the way that we would have liked. Some people can find this quite painful, but the thing to remember here is that it is a learning experience. Being able to tap into what we really felt and thought about a situation is an invaluable experience. We cannot learn by putting up barriers in our own minds or by pretending that things are not as they are. The majority of situations where things haven't gone as you would have liked can be sorted out. Experiencing some sort of discomfort is a sign that you have noticed that things could be done better. It means that you have stayed open to the possibility of other ways of doing things, and that in the future you will be able to learn again. This is good news for the people that you manage and it is good news for the children in your setting – it means that your setting can only benefit from you developing your own practice.

Flexibility

Reflective practitioners are people who are open to the possibility of personal change. There is no point in analysing situations and thinking about how you might approach them differently if you are resistant to changing your own behaviour. Things change – people change and what's considered good practice also changes. Part of a manager's role is to ensure that their setting delivers best current practice, and by using reflective practice we can consider whether our practice is as it should be. Changes in practice will very often mean changes in the way we need to act, and this is, after all, part of our professional development.

Acknowledging personal success

It is important to remember that reflective practice is as much about what goes right as what could have gone better. Strangely enough many people are embarrassed to receive compliments from others. How many people respond to a compliment by saying something like, 'Oh no, I'm not that good at story-telling' instead of 'Thanks – I do enjoy story-telling'? Even stranger perhaps is the fact that many people also find it hard to pay themselves compliments – these people seem to focus on the things that haven't gone so well and pay no attention to their achievements. Reflective practitioners give themselves a pat on the back for things that go well. When things don't go so well they give themselves credit for being brave enough to admit it.

Professional integrity

It is all too easy to take things personally, especially when working with people. People who work in child-centred settings often take great pride and personal satisfaction in their work. It is no wonder then that many of us find it difficult not to take things to heart. Recognising the need to do things differently next time does not make you a bad person – it simply means that you have been professional enough to be able to make an objective assessment of your own behaviour.

Analytical thinking

People working in child-centred settings are often very busy people. Managers of these settings have many different calls on their time and will often be called upon to make 'on the hoof' decisions. Analytical thinking can be very difficult in this sort of environment, yet managers do need to be able to think in a structured way in order to develop their own practice and the work of the setting. Using models such as the five-stage reflective practice model can help to focus thinking in a structured way.

Recognising barriers to reflective practice

Some people find reflective practice easy and others have to work a bit harder at it. This is simply because different people have different ways of thinking, learning and processing information. Those of us to whom reflective practice does not come so easily need to treat it just like another skill to be learnt as part of our management role and one which will take time and practice to develop fully. People can certainly learn to become reflective practitioners, but sometimes when things appear tough or challenging we can put up barriers in order to ward off change. So it is important to recognise and deal with the barriers in order to develop effective reflective practice. Some of the most common barriers we've come across are these:

- 'I'm a doer, not a thinker.'

- 'I've been doing this job for 15 years and there's nothing you can tell me about running a nursery/playgroup/after-school club, etc.'

- 'But I've got enough to do already.'

- 'We're fine / I'm fine / my setting's fine as it is. Nobody has ever told me we're / I'm not / it isn't!'

- 'I just get on with it – analysing it spoils it for me.'

CASE STUDY

Denise is the manager of a nursery. Recently she has had some students working in her setting, and she has found herself becoming increasingly frustrated with the amount of time she has been spending supporting them. The final straw came one day when she asked one of the students to 'wash the dishes' after lunch, and, on returning from a meeting, found that he had done just that. All the dishes were spotless, but the cutlery and cups were still dirty and the kitchen had not been left clean and tidy.

Denise realised that she had been gradually losing her ability to deal with issues in the nursery calmly, so she decided to shut herself away and do a piece of specific reflective practice on this situation. This is what she came up with:

Intention

Denise knew that by asking the student to 'wash the dishes', she had meant him to wash up all the equipment the children had used at lunchtime and to leave the kitchen clean and tidy.

Experience

Denise recalled that she had asked the student to carry out the task while she was in a hurry to get to her meeting.

Action

Denise noticed that, when she was talking to the student, she didn't give him any opportunity to ask questions and she didn't check out what he had actually understood her to mean. She had made an assumption that everybody understood the meaning of the phrase that she used.

Outcome

What had actually happened, much to Denise's frustration, was that the dishes had been washed but the job was not completed.

Development

Denise resolved that, before asking people to carry out tasks again, she would not assume that they knew how to do the job. She would give clearer instructions first and also ask if there was anything else that the person needed to know before she left them to get on with it. She decided to allow more time for setting tasks rather than doing it in a rush. She also decided that there was no point in getting frustrated with the student – she would instead use this as a training opportunity to show him how she wanted the task to be completed.

Putting it into practice

- See reflective practice as a vital part of both your own role and those of all members of your team.

- After doing something that involved some sort of interaction with another person, take just three minutes to think about it before rushing on to the next thing.

- Develop continuous reflective practice by focusing on the interaction which is taking place and noticing what is happening.

- Use the five-stage reflective practice model to focus your reflective practice.

- Put aside time for specific reflective practice at the end of a shift, a day or a session.

- Encourage others to develop their reflective practice by role-modelling the techniques and introducing them into team meetings, supervision, etc.

- Find ways of getting support to develop your own reflective practice.

- Give yourself credit when you are pleased with the results of your reflective practice.

- When reflective practice shows how you could behave differently next time, remember to accept the learning.

CHAPTER 4

Decision-making

Making a decision is simply to choose a course of action from two or more options. This is an everyday part of working in child-centred settings and very often we make decisions without noticing that we are doing so. Practitioners in our field can often be heard talking about 'thinking on our feet', meaning that they have very little time to weigh up the alternatives before making a decision. Managers of child-centred settings are responsible for taking all sorts of decisions, and while some of these will be easily made, others will not. Managers therefore need to develop skills to help them to feel comfortable about making decisions as part of their role.

Essential skills for decision-making

- Confidence
- Time management
- Accepting responsibility
- Professional integrity
- Intuition
- Reflective practice

Why is decision-making an important skill?

There are some managers who find decision-making difficult and regard it as an unwelcome chore rather than an integral and essential part of their job. These managers will put decisions off until it is actually far too late to make them properly, and because they haven't allowed enough time to make decisions, the decisions they do make are usually not very good ones. It is not a coincidence then that the next time they have to make a decision they do not feel very positive about having to do it!

Reasons for not liking decision-making include

- fear of failure, not wanting to 'get it wrong'

- feeling stressed about having to make decisions within a certain time frame

- seeing decision-making as having to 'take sides' and worrying about upsetting people

- perceiving it as a 'waste of time' to use a decision-making process.

However we feel about it, being able to make decisions is a crucial skill for managers who are developing the work of their setting. Without clear decisions, teams will be unclear as to the direction that they are to work in and progress will therefore be slow or non-existent. Misunderstandings can also arise from situations where decisions have been ambiguous, with people getting frustrated because they cannot fully understand the implications of the decision. This can cause tension between individuals and within teams. Frustration can also be caused when too much time is taken over decisions, as other people are very often affected by decision-making and need to know the outcome so that they can put it into practice. Tension and frustration of any kind hamper the work and mean that managers have to use precious time and energy sorting out problems within their team, rather than taking the work of the organisation forward. A lack of any sort of decision-making can mean that the setting gets stuck in a rut. Making clear decisions in good time is therefore crucial to individuals and teams being able to achieve their organisational goal.

Types of decision

There are three different types of decision that managers in child-centred settings are responsible for making. These are day-to-day decisions, operational decisions and development decisions. All of these types require a slightly different approach and set of skills.

Day-to-day practice decisions

These are decisions that need to be taken on most days that the setting is operating. For example, decisions about whether a sick child needs to go home, whether the bins need emptying, whether the rope swing is safe enough until it can be repaired, etc. To make these decisions, managers need a sound knowledge of the setting's policies and procedures, some successful experience in making such judgements, and a bit of faith in their own abilities to make those decisions. In the case of day-to-day practice decisions we go through a simple process, sometimes without even realising it, which is

- establishing the facts

- weighing up the options

- deciding on the course of action.

Effective managers try to delegate as many as possible of these day-to-day practice decisions to other members of the team. Unless your team is very small, there is usually somebody else who, with a bit of support and training, could make decisions about when to order more craft materials and whether it's necessary to bring children inside on a cold winter's evening. By delegating such routine, predictable decisions, managers free up for themselves more time to make the more involved decisions that they are responsible for.

Operational decisions

These are the decisions that affect the quality of practice and provision within the setting; for example, judgements about whether a particular training course is suitable for volunteers, how much of the budget can be spent on replacing new play equipment, which sort of quality assurance scheme is most suitable for the setting, and so on. These decisions can only really be taken by the manager of the setting, who will need to refer to the operational policies and procedures and other documentation in order to make a decision in the best interest of the setting.

There will usually be some parameters involved in operational decisions – in other words, some sort of boundaries within which the manager needs to decide. In the examples above, the parameter for the training course is the content of the course itself; the parameter for replacing the play equipment is the amount of money in the budget; and the parameter for the quality assurance scheme is the content and process of the quality assurance scheme plus factors such as cost, time involved, etc.

It could be said, therefore, that operational decisions are relatively easy to make – there are usually a limited number of options with clear parameters. Again, knowledge, experience and confidence in their decision-making abilities will help managers to be able to make this sort of decision with relative ease.

Development decisions

In contrast to operational decisions, development decisions are those that are more complicated, more involved and usually have no previous examples, models, policies, etc. to follow. There is nothing predictable about development decisions – they are not the sort of decision that managers have to make every day, and when they do need to be made it is usually up to the manager to set their own boundaries. Development decisions are those which will usually result in a major change for the setting and/or the service, and could include, for example,

- whether to take on or lay off staff

- whether to develop the outdoor space and, if so, how

- whether to offer student placements and practice teaching

- whether to take on registered charity status

- whether to change the setting's operating hours

- whether to open another branch of the service.

Some of these examples will, of course, have a precedent. Yet even if this is not the first time that staff have been taken on, the people involved in making the decisions may not be able to draw on previous experience as circumstances may have changed. Managers may therefore need to start 'from scratch', and later in this chapter we will look at a seven-step model which will help you to do that in a logical way.

Managers in child-centred settings need to focus on operational and developmental decisions. It is up to the manager to develop the service, and the ability to make those sorts of decision is one of the things that differentiate managers from non-managers. Managers should take care that they are not just focusing on the day-to-day practice decisions, because it is too easy to get caught up in the daily routine and not actually manage and develop the service.

CASE STUDY (PART 1)

Conrad manages a playbus. Last summer the playbus visited some rural areas and ran some free-play sessions which included children of all ages. The feedback from the children was excellent, and so now they are preparing to run the same sort of sessions again this summer. However, external agencies (some of whom provide funding) are putting pressure on the playbus team to make the sessions more structured and to contain some holiday literacy support. Conrad and the rest of his team feel instinctively that the sessions wouldn't go down so well, and Conrad has to make a decision about how to go forward with the summer project.

Conrad has several options. He can

- go with his and his team's gut feelings, ignore the pressure and carry on with the free-play sessions

- strike a compromise and run mornings as free play and afternoons as literacy support

- turn the whole project into a literacy support scheme.

Conrad doesn't feel comfortable with any of those options and realises that he needs to put some time aside to make this decision.
(To be continued after the next section.)

Seven steps to effective decision-making

Decision-making is best approached as an organised and logical thought process. The more we practise planned and organised decision-making, the easier it becomes. These seven steps are useful in helping us to think about operational decisions and developmental decisions clearly and logically. Remember that we are not suggesting that you use this process for day-to-day practice decisions – nobody would go through this to make a decision about whether the bins need emptying!

1 Define the parameters

There are two boundaries that managers need to be clear about when setting out to make a decision. First of all, it is useful to remind yourself about the organisational aim of your setting. Secondly, you need to be clear as to what it is you are trying to make a decision on. This might sound a bit obvious, but these two parameters will give you a 'bottom line' where no others exist.

2 Collect information

What do you need to know in order to make the decision? You may already feel that you have many facts relevant to your decision in your head, but just to be on the safe side, put them down on paper. This not only means that you can easily check facts when making a decision, but also means that you will be able to feel more confident about having considered the facts. If you need more information, you may need to do some research into the topic, and you will need to build in extra time for this.

3 Identify options

Most decisions will have several possible outcomes. Make a list of all the outcomes that you can think of and then try to come up with a couple more that you wouldn't normally have thought of. Remember that at this stage you are not making a judgement on the options – just write them all down and see what they look like for now.

4 Consider the options and make the decision

One of the best ways to weigh up the options is to set each one against the organisational aim and objectives of the setting. Which option seems to fit most closely with what the service is trying to achieve? Some may immediately appear to go against your aim and can be thrown out straightaway. Others may need a bit more careful consideration and you may have to include judgements about other factors such as resources, legislation and so on in order to weed out some of the rest.

5 Make contingency plans

We do not wish to be too pessimistic about these things, but it is always possible that the decision you made will not turn out to be the one that you would have made with the advantage of hindsight. If it all goes wrong as a result of your decision, it is best to have done some thinking beforehand about how you would handle this situation. It is often the case that decisions need to be made with insufficient information and so it is important to try to anticipate possible outcomes and to consider what you will do about them if they happen.

The simplest and often most effective way of drawing up contingency plans is to list all the things that could go wrong, and against each one write what you would do about it. Then put the list away and forget about it. At least if you do need to manage yourself, your team and your organisation out of a crisis you will have already thought about how to get started and will feel more in control of the situation as a result.

6 Implement the decision

Introduce the decision and put it into place. You will find more on how to do this in Chapter 6.

7 Monitor and evaluate the decision

Decide how long you will monitor for – in other words, how long you will give the decision time to settle down – and then evaluate the decision in the light of the impact it has made on your setting. (You will find more information on how to do this in Chapter 10.) You can also use reflective practice to help you to evaluate your own part in the decision-making process.

CASE STUDY (PART 2)

Conrad puts an afternoon aside to make his decision. He gets out the mission statement of the playbus, which states that the playbus 'aims to provide play opportunities in communities where little or no play provision already exists'. He also reminds himself that he has to make a decision about whether to change the way that the sessions are run to incorporate literacy support. Conrad collects information from the external bodies on what literacy support would involve. He researches the value of free play in children's development by reading some books and doing some research on the web. He also finds the results from the children's evaluation of the last summer project.

He then lists the options that he has identified earlier and wonders if he can come up with any more. He adds the following to his list:

- ask for funding for specialist workers to come on board and run literacy support for those who want it in parallel with the free-play sessions

---

> ● make a presentation to the funders on the value of what we are planning to do and suggest other ways of providing literacy support.
>
> Conrad looks at his list of options and decides that the last one best fits with what the playbus was set up to do. It would also give the playbus a chance to make a more general point about the value of its work. Conrad decides that, in case the external bodies are not convinced enough, he should have the second-to-last option as his contingency plan. If they do have to incorporate an educational aspect, then it can be offered on the basis of choice so that children won't automatically have to miss out on their play opportunities.
>
> Conrad puts his decision into practice by putting a lot of work into his presentation and he asks his team to help him with ideas about what it should contain. Following his presentation he monitors his decision to make the presentation by gauging the response of those present. He does this by asking them whether they feel that making the presentation has been a good idea. He makes his evaluation of whether he has made a good decision based on the results of his monitoring.

Developing your own skills

Accepting responsibility

Managers do have to make decisions and be responsible for the decisions they make. Managers who do not accept full responsibility for making decisions are in danger of something called 'paralysis by analysis'. In other words, they are so worried by the fact that they might not make the best decision that they consider the decision so much that they are unable to make any decision whatsoever. It is true that some decisions will not work out as you would have hoped, but in Chapter 1 we looked at the need to accept imperfection, and this is also true of making decisions. The important thing for a manager is always to accept that a bad decision, as long as it was made properly in the first place, appeared to be the best decision at the time that it was made.

Compromise is a fine technique with which to deal with many situations, but when it comes to making management decisions, it can only be the manager who is responsible for this. Managers should not be tempted to make decisions that are designed to keep two sides of any debate happy. This course of action is not a decision, it is a compromise, and it is important that managers do not mix up the two. After all, it is the manager who is going to be held accountable for any decision that is taken – and so the manager needs to make sure that they have taken a particular line of action for the best reasons.

It is often a good idea to involve others in making decisions. Some positive reasons for involving others are:

● other team members have different knowledge and experience

● team members can feel that being involved in decisions makes them more part of the setting – they feel more included

- team members who have played a part in making a decision which they support will work harder to make it succeed.

However, if managers choose to involve others in making decisions they must be clear (both with themselves and with others) that they are asking for ideas and views. Managers should not ask team members to make the decisions for them.

Some decisions that managers make will prove to be unpopular. Managers may find themselves being challenged about their decisions, either directly or indirectly. Managers need to be confident enough to explain their decisions logically and clearly and to stand by the decisions they have made. If the decision turns out to be less than perfect, managers need to accept responsibility for the decision and to be honest with others about how they would make the decision differently next time.

Professional integrity

Any decision must first and foremost be in line with the organisational aim of the setting and be taken in the light of what the setting wants to achieve. It is inevitable, in any organisation that is focused on and run by people, that personalities will always come into play and sometimes obscure the decision that needs to be made. It is the job of the manager to listen to views and ideas, where they consider it appropriate, and then to steer a clear course through all of those contributions to decide what will best meet the aim of the setting.

Effective managers do not make decisions based on what's good for individuals – they make decisions based on what's best for their setting (even when there are people involved in, or affected by, the decision being taken). Managers in child-centred settings need to be aware that, even when decisions affect or involve people they may be friendly with at work, their job is to make decisions for the good of the children in their setting.

Intuition

John Adair (2002: 53) talks about 'sensing' the effects of the decision as an important part of evaluation. In other words, what does the setting feel like once the decision has been implemented – how do people seem to be coping with the change? Intuition, or 'gut feeling', can play an important part in decision-making, and managers can take into consideration their intuition when making decisions as well as when evaluating them.

It is important to listen to gut feelings – not to rely on them to tell you what decision to make on their own, but to include them in the process as something that could have an impact on the decision. It is also important to remember that it is very difficult to tap into intuition if you are too tired, stressed or worried. The more pressured you feel, the less intuition will be available to you.

Putting it into practice

- Managers do not have to make all the decisions in the setting, even if they are ultimately responsible for them.

- Make a decision about which decisions you should take and which decisions you can pass on to others.

- All decisions should be taken in line with what is best for your setting and ultimately for the children you work with.

- Use intuition to help you to weigh up both sides of the decision.

- Remember that taking a decision is not the same as reaching a compromise.

- Accept that not all decisions will turn out according to plan.

- Be prepared for some of your decisions to be challenged or to be unpopular.

- Use reflective practice to learn from past decisions and to develop your decision-making skills.

CHAPTER 5

Giving feedback

A major part of the manager's role is to give feedback to individuals and the team as a whole. How else will people know whether the job they are doing is of the standard required and meeting the objectives of the setting?

However, feedback is often misconstrued as the manager's chance to say what they want and to inform individual team members what they are doing is wrong. Effective management processes include times when feedback is given that is neither of these things. Nor is it a formal evaluation – that is covered in Chapter 10. Feedback is the process by which a manager states their aims and objectives, opinions and thoughts on a given topic/idea/suggestion/action/task to a team member to assist that individual in their work and to make clear the overall aims of the setting. A manager has the right to inform people of changes that need to take place and the team has the right to be informed. An effective feedback process allows this to happen.

Essential skills for giving feedback

- Understanding the different methods of giving feedback
- Preparing and planning
- Understanding expectations
- Being aware of the basic 'do's' and classic 'don'ts' when giving feedback
- Giving objective criticism
- Giving praise
- Receiving feedback

Why is feedback important?

It is a manager's job to make sure that the team are doing what they are supposed to be doing according to their job description and required duties. If you don't, who will? Managers who offer regular feedback opportunities for teams and for children at the setting are creating an atmosphere where issues of concern, ideas and suggestions can be valued and used to make improvements. It is also an opportunity to explain a process, working practice or procedure and to look at individual ways of working with the idea of praising good practice and stopping poor practice. Teams will feel better about asking for feedback from a manager if the feedback is objective and fair.

Effective, objective feedback can

- highlight good practice

- prevent or stop poor practice

- build self-esteem and confidence

- build good relationships

- show individuals they are valued and supported

- deal with potential conflicts before they develop

- assist in providing a quality setting to children

- enable a manager to obtain information from a user or team member.

A manager can assist people in their own development through their work and improve their performance through feedback effectively delivered. The responsibility for this requires the manager to plan and prepare carefully so that the end result is not a team member or team feeling humiliated or put down. There are a range of skills that a manager can develop to do this.

Developing your own skills

Having looked at why we need to give feedback, the rest of the chapter describes the skills managers can develop and practise so that feedback becomes a useful process in the development of the whole team, including the manager.

Different methods

There are a number of ways of offering feedback to a team and managers can use several methods alongside one another. Decide which is most appropriate to the individual team member and the type of feedback to be given; we have listed a few methods to assist you:

Method 1
Regular supervision sessions with individual team members.

Method 2
Regular team meetings with agenda items on tasks and responsibilities that allow feedback from everyone.

Method 3
Review meetings with a set purpose of reviewing how certain projects or ideas are progressing.

Method 4
Annual or biannual team appraisal sessions with a formalised process of logging feedback which each party prepares beforehand, followed by discussions during the meeting on targets, responsibilities, training needs, and any issues of concern.

Method 5
Informal discussions where the manager can give and receive feedback as the team are working.

Choosing a method

The method chosen will depend on what the team and/or individuals are working on. Project work, such as organising the repainting of the building, will require daily or weekly feedback for both the manager and the team.

Individual feedback is best given in one-to-one supervision (method 1), which should happen regularly – at least once every month (these supervision sessions are about daily tasks and responsibilities and will incorporate personal performance); **and** in annual team appraisal sessions (method 4), when more medium- and long-term goals can be discussed and agreed. If a manager has to give objective criticism about an individual's performance, both the supervision and team appraisal methods are more effective than catching people on the hop when their attention is focused on something else.

If a manager wishes to give the whole team feedback on their joint performance and/or practice, use method 2 or 3. It may be because the manager is unsure of who is holding a project up, or the whole team have adopted a way of working which is ineffectual or shows poor practice (team meetings would allow a group discussion and enable the manager to hear why the team are not working as they should), or the whole team has done very well and it is a collective praising that is required.

Managers who have good working relations with the team will naturally give feedback on a daily basis wherever possible in normal day-to-day conversations (method 5).

Remember feedback is a two-way process: a manager must be prepared to listen and receive feedback also. We explore giving and receiving feedback later on in the chapter.

Preparation and planning

There is an adage that says, 'Always think before you speak.' If we apply this to how managers give feedback it is strongly advised that feedback they wish to impart is prepared. Managers need to reflect on what end result they want. Telling someone off gives us power momentarily, it may relieve pent-up emotions for a little while and satisfy our ego as manager but ultimately it will not get the job done well or encourage that team member to change their practice or attitude. We need to develop confidence (see Chapter 1), and personal skills to do this well and to be aware of when we as managers are not being clear or honest.

Think about why you are giving the feedback, who the feedback is to, what the effects of the feedback could be and what you want from the process, and how best to deliver the feedback. A useful way of remembering this is

Subject, Receiver, Outcome, Mode = SROM.

CASE STUDY

Latitia as deputy manager of a large nursery had to give feedback to Eileen, who was not answering the door or the phone to parents in a courteous or friendly manner. This had been raised in a general discussion during a team meeting where she had hoped that Eileen would pick up on it. Latitia planned to raise the matter during a weekly supervision session and used the acronym above to help her plan.

She knew the Subject was about working with parents and how the nursery was perceived by them; she knew that Eileen was good with the children, friendly and helpful with other colleagues but not always mindful of her own way of communicating. She anticipated that Eileen (Receiver) would be embarrassed and probably defensive when she mentioned this, so she thought the Outcome had to be that she would be made aware and shown what was expected of her so that she could practise it. Latitia felt the best way of doing this (Mode) was to sandwich what she had to say between some praise of Eileen's recent work with the children and then to ask Eileen for her own thoughts on the work with parents, e.g. 'Where do you think you could make an impact?' Latitia wrote some questions down that she would ask Eileen, as well as the points that she wanted to make.

If giving criticism, remember it is a **constructive** event **not** a negative one. In giving feedback that involves criticism of performance, a manager is creating the opportunity for discussion and self-reflection; it is not an end in itself but is done to achieve another goal.

Preparing

- Write a list of key points.

- Do not make more than three points whether they are praise or criticism – it can be too much to take on and 'muddy' the thinking of the receiver and be less effective.

- Think about the receiver: how are they going to 'hear' what you are saying? Are they uncomfortable receiving praise or criticism? How can you make it easier? Are you giving thanks and praise or are you illustrating poor practice or a negative attitude?

- Make the points specific.

- Write down some examples to give in the feedback.

- Think of positive things the team member has also done.

- Make a list of reasons or background information that support your criticism and/or praise – brief notes will do.

- Do not attack the person; comment on their actions and behaviour.

Planning

- Think about the best time of day to give feedback.

- Write a memo to the team about the feedback session, giving details, or if it is at a team meeting add it to the agenda.

- Think about where the feedback will take place – some managers do not have a separate office in which to hold meetings and so a private, quiet place somewhere else will be needed if you are having a one-to-one discussion.

- If you believe it may be a difficult session, have some water or tea/coffee ready. Allow more time, and do not plan it for the end of the day, as the person would go home without having time to assimilate what you have said and, possibly, sound other colleagues out.

Understanding expectations

In looking at the case study above there are several possibilities to explain Eileen's behaviour and attitude, one being that she may believe that dealing with parents is not her job or her responsibility – her expectation may be that the manager always deals with parents. The manager's expectation, however, is likely to be that all staff deal with parents as and when required and always courteously. In a high-pressured environment, with much going on, individual expectations about how tasks, issues, situations are dealt with can develop and lead the team into a dysfunctional way of working.

By expressing clear expectations – and we are talking about the ones beyond the tasks outlined in the job description – and reinforcing these through feedback sessions or other opportunities, a manager can eradicate false expectations.

Feedback do's and don'ts

A little thought should be given to ways of imparting what you have to say. A common failure in management is that the manager will just want to say what they have to say and not think about **how** they are going to do it. The end result can be devastating and, needless to say, ineffective as the team will not know if the work they are doing meets expectations.

Look at your own motives. Why are you giving the praise or the criticism? Could it be that the team have not understood what is expected of them because you did not make it clear, or they had not had sufficient training to do a certain task, or had not been given clear guidelines, or had come from another setting that never did what you now expect?

Here are some straightforward do's and don'ts when giving feedback:

DO

- Sit as relaxed as you can be and sit opposite if you can.

- Maintain eye contact.

- Use 'I' statements such as 'I liked', 'I have noticed'.

- Keep the tone matter-of-fact.

- Introduce the topic in an appropriate way: 'I wanted to . . .', 'I feel we ought to discuss . . .'

- Keep it factual – point out exactly what it is you are happy with/not happy with.

- Give reasons/background briefly.

- Ask for suggestions or solutions if giving criticism of practice.

- Be firm if the action/behaviour has been repeated.

- Get a response by asking, 'Do you realise . . .?' 'Have you noticed . . .?'

- Summarise – 'So let's agree that you will . . .'

- Keep notes on the meeting, write them up and give a copy to the team member to check and agree; keep a copy of their agreement of the notes on file, especially if you have given feedback on poor practice and asked for changes.

- Be fair.

DON'T

- Rush the session/feedback.

- Attack the person, e.g. 'You are a lazy person.'

- Use negative tone or body language.

- Be put off by aggressive body language and/or tone.

- Be put off by silence: ask open questions to get them talking, offer a beginning of an answer to help them if they are truly stuck – usually due to strong emotions.

- Glare at them.

- Do other things at the same time.

- Be insincere in your praise.

- Threaten: use legitimate organisational procedures to point out the course of action you will have to take.

- Use phrases such as 'It's your own fault.'

- Hide behind your organisation or other people, e.g. 'the management committee think they know everything and want me to get the team to . . .'

Giving praise

When people have done well they like to hear it, especially from someone in authority. Some people have been brought up with the belief that it is embarrassing when someone thanks them, that it means they are obligated to someone, it is a 'soppy' thing to do, and they can feel quite uncomfortable hearing someone thanking them. In addition some managers have a misconception that praising an individual or a team will result in a too relaxed atmosphere and no work will get done, the 'team are only doing what they are paid for' or ' they think "I" want something'. Not necessarily so.

Acknowledgement is important. Humans learn as much from success as from mistakes. By offering thanks, approval, commendation, managers are supporting the individual, acknowledging their good practice and raising their confidence, thus benefiting the individual and the setting. Managers who reflect on their own experiences can see when someone saying 'thank you' has given them self-worth and a sense of satisfaction. The opposite is also true: when managers have experienced not being thanked for the work they have done, feelings of being taken for granted can grow, motivation is reduced, and work can suffer. On the other hand, heaping huge amounts of praise onto someone can sound insincere and they will not respect the next feedback or take the manager seriously.

Do not be put off by someone brushing off what you say; it is largely due to embarrassment and false beliefs. However, if you know someone is very uneasy about being thanked, take them to one side instead of offering it in a group setting, but acknowledge the work briefly in the team meeting, e.g. 'Hafiz's work on the mural outside has really brightened up the place, don't you agree?' Deliver praise in a manner you know will be understood.

Think about who the praise is for, keep it sincere, give examples of what was good or successful and do not 'waffle'. By making the praise specific a manager is giving information to the receiver about what is good so that they can repeat it. In addition, do not sound apologetic – 'I hope you do not mind me saying . . .' will make it sound insincere – or put yourself down when you need to assert yourself – 'If only I had your skills . . .' can be misconstrued as sarcasm.

> **CASE STUDY: GIVING PRAISE**
>
> Latitia was showing a prospective parent around the nursery and witnessed a member of her team running story time with the use of a puppet and a drum. The children were enthralled with the story and joining in with the puppet on cue. When the parent had gone, Latitia made a point of going back into the room to speak to the member of staff to give her feedback: 'The story session seemed to be going very well; I loved the use of the puppet and the drum to keep the children's attention. Well done!'

Giving objective criticism

Criticism can be negative or positive and both types can be received in the same way if the 'ground' is not prepared first. At some stage a manager will have to pass on information to a member of a team that is not going to be easily received. This could be due to outside influences such as OFSTED requirements or a change of policy, or due to poor performance/bad practice. The latter can range from a member of team not pulling their weight to someone who is continually late.

Managers who avoid dealing with the issue of poor performance/bad practice will face conflict at some stage. Managers who blame the individual solely, and/or take it personally that the team member has not done well, will be ineffective in obtaining the goal of objective criticism. The goal is to change an individual or team performance or attitude to the work.

Objective criticism is aimed at the actions, attitude or behaviour, not at the person, as stated above. For example, 'Mai chi, you are always laid back; is that why you are late?' This attacks the person and then says what the behaviour is.

By telling them how they have affected the general work of the team, and/or their own responsibilities, the manager can show how an individual's actions play a major part in team dynamics. Managers should not presume that the individual has remembered a previously agreed point, or that the individual is solely to blame. Expressing criticisms objectively by using facts helps to ensure feedback is not taken as a personal attack. Describing as clearly as possible what the manager is not happy with or what the complaint is about will help the team member see what they are being asked to change.

Why people do not 'hear' criticisms

There are a number of ways that individuals react to receiving criticism of their work. Here are a few:

- they take it personally – 'I am always being got at'

- they flatly deny they had anything to do with the concerns being raised

- they blame others – 'my husband's car, it broke down and then the bus was late'

- they do not hear fully what you are saying because they only have negative experiences of feedback.

Some pointers to help with the above four reactions when giving negative feedback:

1 By introducing the issues without too many details, a manager can ease the situation for the receiver; after all, they may not have any idea of what they have done that is not acceptable or why they are about to receive criticism of their work. By giving brief and clear reasons for raising the issues of concern a manager can support their points of criticism and it will not be seen as a personality clash/ personal dislike, etc.

2 It is important that there is agreement on the criticisms raised (remember, no more than three points). By asking 'open' questions a manager can check that the person has agreed with the issues raised, and giving time for the other person to respond allows the manager the chance to hear information that may be new to them. In cases where this happens the manager must modify the criticism and if necessary withdraw it. (An open question is one where you get more than yes/no in reply, e.g. 'Can you tell me how you feel the activity went?')

3 A manager should always ask the individual if they have any ideas for resolving the situation. Owning the solution can help the individual not only accept the criticism, but also feel they can improve their behaviour. It will also bring up any difficulties that they may be experiencing that impact on their performance and have resulted in the type of feedback now being given.

4 The final stage is summarising the agreed action to be implemented by the team member and placing a time limitation on when this will be achieved by.

In addition to the points above, use steps in Do's and Don'ts to guide you through preparing and giving criticism of team performance. Always think before acting, diagnose the situation first, and remember the person's previous performance and competence before launching in with criticisms.

Receiving feedback

It is just as important for a manager to receive feedback as it is to give it. A manager will want to hear what their team feel and think about the work they do and the way that they are being managed. It also builds good relationships within the setting by allowing issues and ideas to be aired.

As mentioned before, a manager's own experience will have an impact on how they receive feedback from the team and indeed children. Some hints for receiving criticism are given here:

- If you are unclear what the criticism is about, ask for clarification and for an example. Avoid aggression such as 'You haven't got an example, have you?'; try saying it another way: 'I would find it helpful if you could give me some examples of that.'

- If criticism is given aggressively in the form of a personal attack, do not respond likewise; rather separate, if possible, what the criticism is about from the personal references. It may be necessary to point out to the other person that their approach has been very personal and you feel attacked.

- If you do not agree with the criticism, say so. However, do not do this aggressively and dismiss what the other person is saying altogether; rather encourage dialogue: 'So what you are saying is . . .'

- Look at the broader picture: are there issues not being mentioned here that are the root cause of the criticism? For example, have you not done something that you had agreed to do?

- As in the process of giving effective feedback, summarise with the person and suggest some action points you both can agree on. Use 'I' statements throughout to keep this objective.

Make room at team meetings to hear what the team have to say, ask them for ideas or suggestions over plans or actions that you may have to take. Structure the supervision sessions so team members know they can have their say.

Putting it into practice

- Spend a little time thinking about when you want to give feedback and what the best method of doing so is.

- Develop your own confidence in giving feedback by practising.

- Plan and prepare before you give feedback – think who the receiver is, what you want from this exchange, what the best mode of communication is.

- Remember to find something to mention that's positive before giving the negative and always finish on a positive.

- Check personal feelings and thoughts – 'Am I doing this for me?'

- Practise the things you want to say by writing them down in different ways, then choose the best way for the individual/s you are giving feedback to.

- Be aware of the defence systems we as humans use; ask the individual if they have understood or agree with what you have said.

- Be open to others' feedback on you; this may be useful to you in developing your own skills and experience.

- Always write down feedback that you may need to refer to another time.

- Remember you as a manager have the right and the duty to give feedback to the team to get the job done.

CHAPTER 6

Change management

The term 'change management' refers to a carefully planned process of making changes to either a part or all of the way an organisation operates. Change should always occur within an organisation in order to achieve something which will help to achieve the organisational goal. The change process is usually developed and led by a manager in the organisation, and it takes place over a period of time which will vary according to what sort of changes are being made.

It could be argued that managers in child-centred settings have an even harder task than most other managers when it comes to making changes. In a field which has traditionally been seen as a people-centred, caring profession, it can be hard for managers to make changes when they know that their team members and others may be personally affected by those changes – and not always for the better. We can all no doubt think of a time when we have been affected by change and probably can remember thinking that the change should have been made either faster or slower, or perhaps with more communication. Change management is one of the hardest parts of any manager's role. Whether managing a car factory or a children's home, ensuring that change happens (and that it takes place successfully) requires managers to invest a great deal of time and energy in the process.

Essential skills for managing change

- Confidence

- Vision

- Analytical thinking

- Planning

- Understanding individual responses to change

- Time management

- Leadership
- Giving feedback
- Monitoring and evaluation

Why is it important to manage change?

There are, of course, ways of making change happen in organisations that do not involve managing the process. Many managers, perhaps those who do not feel comfortable themselves with change or confident in their abilities to effect change, will simply tell their teams that a change has been put into place and leave the team to get on with it. While change management may look and feel like a long-drawn-out process, managers in child-centred settings can use it to help their team feel supported and valued through the process. The additional benefit will be that the change is more likely to happen and improvements to the service will be made. It can also help you to ensure that not too many changes are being made at one time, as this can be detrimental to achieving progress.

Managing change needs to be approached like any other sort of project, with careful planning, a clear programme of events that need to happen, involvement of others and more time than you probably originally thought it would take. Change cannot and will not happen overnight, and if you try to force change without treating the process like a separate piece of work, it may not happen at all. The other possible outcome of not managing change is that you will not achieve what you planned to achieve, and this could result in unhappy and disappointed team members. It is also possible that, in any change process, things will happen during, or as a result of, the change that you had not envisaged. Like any other project, contingency plans need to be put into place well in advance.

Another issue for managers to take into account when planning change is that to make changes within an organisation often means that you need to attempt to change the people within it. Changing their work practice requires them to examine and change their ideas, their values, their beliefs, and sometimes even their worldview. They may have to revise long-held and cherished ideas and attitudes and they may have to move out of their 'comfort zone' in order to begin new ways of working. None of this is easy for anybody to do in any circumstances. In a work situation where change is not an option, individuals can sometimes feel a huge amount of pressure to change in a relatively short space of time. This can cause stress for the individual and disruption in the setting, especially if an individual cannot see the point of the changes that have been planned. A carefully managed change process can take account of the time and support people will need to change, and is therefore likely to get more effective results than change which is simply imposed on people.

It is important to be aware that most types of change will involve extra resources of some description. Managing a change process will enable you to make plans for additional resources and to think about how you will provide these. Types of extra resources you and your team might need (both during the change process and possibly once the change has taken place) include

- time

- money

- staff cover

- equipment

- outside support or expertise (for example, building advice, legal help).

Finally, it is worth repeating that change should always happen in line with what the organisational aim sets out to achieve. Sometimes it is easy to forget that the purpose of change is to develop the service provided by the organisation. Change should never be introduced because a manager is bored or feels that changing things will help them to assert themselves in the setting. Ensuring that there is a clear link between the proposed change and the development of the setting will mean that change is more likely to be successful.

Internal and external influences

There are two types of factor which cause change in child-centred settings – internal influences and external influences.

Internal influences could include:

- children requesting changes in the way things are done

- team members identifying that a change in practice is needed

- budgetary or funding issues (i.e. too much or not enough money)

- parents suggesting changes

- management identifying areas where things should be done differently

- a decision being taken to expand the service.

External influences may include:

- legislation changes

- requirements to comply with a quality assurance scheme

- OFSTED or other inspectors identifying areas for change

- technology being updated

- competition – a new nursery opens down the road, a local-authority-subsidised after-school club offers cheaper sessions, etc.

- funding bodies changing how they operate and what they will give money for.

To some extent, internal influences can be managed more easily. Managers can usually be more in control of deadlines and can therefore decide on the appropriate timescale in which to make the change. With external influences there is often more pressure to make the changes in a pre-determined length of time (because, for example, the Health and Safety Officer is coming back in three weeks' time, or because a piece of legislation has already come into force). Both types of change require careful planning, although managers need to recognise that external influences can lead to more stress and worry, both for themselves and for the rest of the team.

Four-stage model of change management

Managers and everybody else involved in a change process need to be very clear about what that process will involve. There is a simple four-stage model which can be useful in helping to plan and to keep track of the progress of change:

- Analysis
- Planning
- Implementation
- Monitoring and evaluation.

We discuss analysis and planning in more depth in the section on 'developing your own skills' later in this chapter.

Implementation of the plan should start on the planned start date and by then everybody should have been informed individually as well as in groups and individual concerns should have been addressed. By the start of the plan everybody should also be aware of their new roles and competent to take them on.

The change process can be monitored and evaluated in several ways. These could include:

- how effective the plan was
- how much impact the change has made
- whether the aim of the plan has been achieved
- how people involved in the process feel about the change.

Monitoring and evaluation could be done on more than one occasion, depending on the length of the change process – for example, you may want to monitor how people feel about the change just before it happens, while it's happening, just after it has happened and six months after it has happened.

There is a final stage to the process which you may like to add if things go according to plan – and that is celebration! As we've already said, many people find change hard, and some sort of acknowledgement or even reward during and after the change process will not only be a great motivator but will also show team members that their efforts have been appreciated.

Developing your own skills

Analytical thinking

By analytical thinking we mean being able to think about an issue in a rational, logical way. This type of thinking also involves some sort of detachment from whatever it is that you need to think about, which means being able to step back and consider the issue objectively. This can be quite hard to do, because we all have our own personal biases in the way that we see things at work. In child-centred settings it is common for managers to have made some sort of emotional investment in the way things have been set up or the way things work, and this emotional investment can naturally cloud our judgement as to what the true picture is. A useful skill therefore, analytical thinking helps us to make decisions and judgements with as much unbiased information to hand as possible.

Before they begin to plan the way things are going to change, managers need to understand the way things are in their setting now. This may sound a little odd, because everybody takes it for granted that they know how their setting works. However, what's needed at the start of any change management process is an objective view of what goes on in your setting. Here are some questions that you might find helpful to think about.

What is acceptable and what isn't?

By this we don't mean what do your policies say, but how do things get treated in practice? What, for example, is the general attitude to turning up late for work? How creative are people when it comes to solving problems – or do they always come to you for the answers? Do people turn a blind eye to personal phone calls? Is babysitting for parents allowed and, if it isn't, does it go on anyway?

What spoken and unspoken rules exist?

For example, is it assumed that if a parent is late then somebody will stay with the child (rather than putting their coat on and leaving you with the child every time)? Does everybody always go on social outings and, if people don't go, do they get left out of general discussions during work time? Is there a hierarchy – June always collects the fees because she is most senior, for example (even though in practice there is no reason why any of the team members can't collect the fees)? Is it 'accepted practice' that Dave is the 'craft expert' and nobody else does craft with the children?

By asking these types of question and looking objectively at the answers you should begin to draw up a picture of your setting and your team in terms of how receptive to change they are.

Management theory suggests that you are more likely to succeed in bringing about effective change if the culture of the organisation can be preserved. For example, if your analysis tells you that your setting is used to routine and it doesn't rely on people being creative to deliver the service, you need to bear this in mind when planning your change. If change involves putting into place something which is routine and predictable, you will have less resistance and therefore more chance of the change succeeding. If the change requires people to be more creative both during and after the change process, however, then you will have to allow extra time and support for this in your planning. If you are going to try to change the culture of the organisation, then you need first to ensure that people feel comfortable with the change before the change actually takes place – after all, you are about to move them out of their comfort zone.

Planning

Managers need to draw up written plans for putting the change into effect and the plan should include:

- the goal you are aiming to achieve through the change process (see Chapter 2 for more on this topic)

- the timescale over which the change will take place and what will happen when – this needs to be very specific so you can monitor your progress, e.g. 15 May, team meeting. The timescale should also have a clear start and finish date.

- who will be involved in the change and how they will be consulted and involved in the process

- the resources you already have and additional resources you will need

- any budgetary/financial implications

- who will be involved in leading and managing the change and what their roles will be in the process – it is sometimes possible for people in the team to be involved in supporting you and for them to take on some of the work

- the key stages involved in the timescale and what contingencies you will put into place if these have not been achieved

- communication details – who gets to know what and when. This is crucial – not having a clear plan to disseminate information can lead to rumours and gossip which can hinder the change process.

- how the change will be monitored and evaluated

- how achieving the change will be celebrated, both the small steps along the way and the whole project.

CASE STUDY

Inspired by a training course, Sonia went back to her playcentre that evening and took a good hard look at the way that the setting was laid out. She thought about what she had learnt on the course and could see how to make the centre

---

much more child-friendly. When everybody had gone home, Sonia stayed behind for several hours until late at night, moving furniture, throwing out broken toys, changing notice boards and completely revamping the whole setting so that it looked completely different.

Pleased with the results, Sonia eagerly looked forward to her team's arrival and appreciation the next day when they came in to set up. However, she was very disappointed and quite cross at the reaction of the team. John arrived, made no comment about everything being in a different place but did swear on several occasions when he couldn't find anything. Amel arrived and didn't say anything about the changes. She just kept wandering around, not doing anything, as if she didn't know where she was any more. Doug got to work and commented to the other two that some people obviously didn't have enough work to do if they had time to move furniture around.

When the children arrived they were surprised to see that things weren't where they had been yesterday. Some of them said that they liked the messy play better on the floor but Sonia did notice that the children were more disruptive than usual.

Sonia felt that all her hard work had been for nothing and her team were obviously not happy with her. The atmosphere in the centre was not good and the children picked up on this, which in turn caused more friction.

Understanding individual responses to change

Not everybody has a negative reaction to change, but many people do, and the reasons for this are many and varied. Before embarking on any sort of change process, managers need to be aware of the reasons for individuals feeling negative about change and to develop strategies for combating the negativity. Reasons for dislike of change include:

- not understanding why change is necessary ('if it ain't broke, don't fix it')

- being too busy getting on with the job (this is particularly the case in child-centred settings where there are a lot of 'doers'!)

- the change involving a real or perceived threat

- the individual having allegiances within the setting, which means that they are going to resist whatever you do, change included

- fear of loss of control / insecurity about what the change will mean in the future

- worries about increased workload

- concerns about hidden agendas – 'This can't just be about changing the shift pattern; she must be trying to get rid of me.'

- uncertainty about their role during and after the change.

Managers need to identify the cause(s) of resistance to change in individuals, and then work out how to put to rest the fears and concerns of each person. When people are feeling worried and insecure, it is tempting for managers to 'beat around the bush' in an attempt to try to shield individuals from more aggravation. However, this course of action will generally cause more worry and insecurity, as the person concerned will sense that something isn't right and then think that there is more to the issue than there actually is. Managers need to be able to talk through the fact they think the person is unhappy about the proposed change, listen to any fears or concerns the individual might have and address those worries one by one (see Chapter 5).

Managers need to remember that dealing with change can be a very personal experience and that different people will need different levels of support at different times. People who are positive about change will also need support, as they too will be affected by change.

Managers are human beings too and will have their own individual responses to change which they need to be aware of and deal with. It is advisable for managers involved in change management to get some support themselves, because when driving forward any kind of change it is important to stay focused and positive throughout. There may be times when it's hard and you feel like giving up, but it is vital to hold on to your vision and the fact that, if you don't lead the way, your setting will not develop in the way you feel that it should.

Leadership

When planning to make changes, it is essential to work out how you will take people with you. In a child-centred setting this could mean your team, your managers, the parents, the children, external bodies – some or all of these may be involved, depending on the sort of change you are making. In the case study above, Sonia was obviously excited about making changes and this was really positive. However, carried away by her enthusiasm, she forgot that as a manager her role was not to make the change herself, but to inspire and lead others in making the change together. Ways that managers can help people to feel more positive about change include:

- involving the individual in the change process if they want to be involved
- holding discussions about the need for change and asking for people's views on the proposed change
- addressing individual fears and concerns
- reminding them of the vision of a better service and going over the reasons for change
- organising formal or informal training if the concerns are about lack of skills and/or knowledge
- selling the change – point out not only the benefits for others but also the benefits for them.

CASE STUDY

Sue, the manager of a small nursery chain, had been aware for some time that the separate settings did not work together. In fact, it seemed to her that the managers in each setting did just about everything they could to work in isolation, rather than being part of the bigger team. When she visited some of the settings, she overheard negative conversations about the other sites, and there was apparently much jealousy and rivalry between the settings over such things as resources and venues.

Sue knew that things had to change and wrote down what she would like to achieve: 'To ensure that all the nurseries work together in promoting a corporate identity in the next nine months.'

Over the next month she spent more time in each of the nurseries, listening and observing how things were done in each one. She learnt that each nursery had its own culture, but also that they all basically believed in the work that they were doing and wanted the best for the children in their care.

At the end of the month, Sue drew up her plan to implement change. She set the following objectives to help her to meet her aim:

- arrange some training for staff from all the sites on the value of the work they were doing with the children. She felt that this would boost morale and help staff members to find common ground and see that they were all working towards the same thing. She would also organise a buffet lunch to make staff feel valued and attend the session herself, so that she could introduce the change to all of the staff at the same time.

- review the budget for each setting and to share the information with all the managers. She would involve the managers in the review so they could have an open discussion about whether resources were fairly allocated.

- explain to the managers, prior to the training day, her vision for change on a one-to-one basis so that they could air any concerns. She recognised that the managers were key to selling her vision of a service which was coherent and cohesive.

- arrange for all the managers to be trained together on corporate identity. She would ask them to bring what they had learned to a meeting to discuss how to take it forward.

- arrange, in conjunction with the managers, job swaps for nursery nurses amongst the sites.

- hold weekly management meetings to enable managers to keep her informed about how the job swaps, etc. were going. She hoped that by doing this she would encourage the managers to ask staff what they had learnt and how they had got on.

- review all the policies, procedures and publicity and ask a group of staff made up from all the sites to work with her in order to standardise the documents. She felt that not only was this a good way of getting staff to work together but it would also mean that a clear picture should emerge of the similarities and differences between the sites.

> Sue noted in her plans that there might be budgetary implications if she needed to close sites in order to get training done, but she decided that, as this wasn't a regular event and it was very important, it was all right to do this.

Putting it into practice

- Making any sort of change in a setting needs to be carefully planned and managed.

- Be honest and realistic about where you are starting from and the pace at which you can reasonably expect change to take place.

- Remember that some people will welcome change and others will find it more difficult, so plans need to include ways of keeping everybody on board with the change.

- Address individual concerns and fears about change throughout the change process.

- Use the vision of the benefits the change will bring for the setting, the children and the team to help you to lead the team through the change.

- Make sure that your plan includes additional resources you will need, both during the change process and once the change has taken place.

- Keep everybody informed about progress and give positive feedback to individuals as well as to the group.

- Celebrate small successes during the change process as well as the final achievement of the whole project.

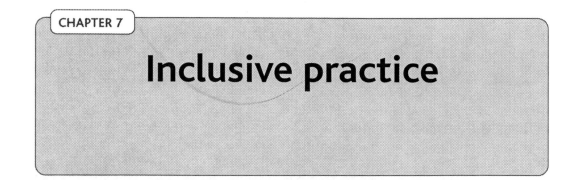

CHAPTER 7

Inclusive practice

'By the time we are 5 or 6 years old, 99.9% of people will have experienced some form of prejudice' (J. Guillebeaux, 'Inspire' Conference, 2002).

Discrimination must be dealt with in all aspects of society and especially in services to children and their families. This means raising awareness, acknowledging differences, challenging barriers and opposition but, more importantly, every adult working with children and young people learning to be a consistent, positive role model.

Essential skills for developing inclusive practice

- Creating a climate of openness and tolerance

- Keeping up to date

- Raising awareness

- Understanding language and terminology

- Interactions and interventions

Why is developing inclusive practice important?

Society changes all the time and has done for centuries. The diversity of other cultures mixing with current ones adds a richness that can and does benefit all. Central to child-centred settings is the role of all workers in ensuring equality of opportunity and implementation of anti-discriminatory procedures when providing a place to play and learn – not just for some children but for *all* children and throughout *all* opportunities. This is what we mean by inclusive practice.

All children are different, of course. Different *does not* mean bad, not worthy, less able, but prejudices have resulted in attitudes towards differences that encourage people to believe a particular group of people are better than another, or a particular person is better than another, rather than all people being different, which adds to the interest of living with other humans.

A manager has the right to make sure that an individual team member's attitudes are not discriminatory towards the children, the parents or the other members of the team. An individual's attitude and approach will have a direct effect on their practice because of their own childhood experiences and deeply held beliefs and, possibly, attitudes that have never been examined. Being aware of our own history and where some of our beliefs come from will help to make us more tolerant of change or differences. For a manager of a team providing a positive caring environment for children, ensuring good practice with regard to implementation of inclusive policies, looking at approaches and procedures with the team is essential if children are to learn themselves about positive behaviour towards others.

No society at the moment is free from inequalities; a manager's role is to make sure that they and the team create an environment where children can reach their full potential without discriminating barriers. It is as simple as recognising *within yourself* that experiences have an impact on emotions and thoughts and, with this awareness, creating a balance in your approach and attitude to be a positive role model.

Developing your own skills

Much of the manager's responsibilities with regard to inclusive practice will focus on monitoring behaviour, attitudes and procedures, plus supporting team members or children in understanding effective ways of responding to inappropriate remarks or behaviour. If part of your vision is to make your child-centred setting more inclusive, how you and your team actively encourage positive relationships will be vital to realising this vision.

Responsibility for making decisions and pushing forward any changes by taking necessary actions at appropriate times lies largely with the manager. So a manager's own understanding of how to be, what kind of role model they are, supports the whole process for the team and the children. Any incongruity will undermine the actions you are taking. So start with yourself!

Creating a climate of openness and tolerance

It is not possible to know and understand everything about all the different cultures and heritages that make up the backgrounds of the children and young people of the British Isles or indeed those using your setting, so **ask**. It is better to encourage an atmosphere where people **enquire and do not assume**, where people are learning from each other and trying to understand, than to develop prejudices on grounds of ignorance or to develop avoidance reactions. By keeping up to date with information on the children using your setting and encouraging children and team members to be open-minded you will be able to create a climate of openness and tolerance.

The role of a manager will include being open and frank with parents and children, if what is being asked is not possible and would go against policies of the service. For example, if a parent asks that their child does not eat certain foods for religious or health reasons, complying with this request is usually easy. On the other hand, if a parent asks that their daughter, aged 11, no longer be allowed to play on adventure playground equipment because it is not 'ladylike', that would be a request to question because it is discriminating against her on grounds of gender. This would be against the setting's policy on equality. A manager needs to safeguard the rights of the child in this case because it is unlikely that she will be able to do so for herself.

Keeping up to date

A full understanding of inclusive practice will require a manager to know what 'equality' means both legally and in best practice terms. Hyacinth Malik (1998: 3) gives the definition as

- valuing a diverse, multicultural, multilingual and multiracial society

- valuing individuals, genders, disabilities, cultures, religions and lifestyles

- offering and providing equal chances to everyone in society, irrespective of variation within the population

- not endorsing the concept of superiority and inferiority within and amongst the population

- maintaining and upholding each individual's human right not to be discriminated against and denied their equality

- recognising that there is a variety of child-rearing practices which are all equally effective in providing security for children.

Another role is managing the policies and procedures of the setting. However, managers are not just in charge of writing and reviewing the policies and procedures although that is essential to good practice and is a requirement by law under the Children Act 1989. By using the team, advice from the local SENCO (see section on do's and don'ts below), and in some cases children – no matter what their age, all children can be involved – a great deal can be learnt from sharing information in ways of dealing with sexism, racism, stereotyping, etc. Team meetings or specially arranged focus discussions on inclusion – who is not included in society, the reasons why this might be and what can be done to change this – will allow views to be heard and in some cases questioned. Discussing policies helps the team and you focus on what your setting believes is captured in your vision.

A manager must make sure the policies show that children and the team are not discriminated against because of race, gender, disability, age, culture or language. The policy needs to say more than 'we will not discriminate against a person because of their race, culture, disability, etc'; it will need to specify **how** the setting will not discriminate and **how** you are developing practices that are inclusive. Use the policy as a foundation for creating inclusivity for all, as stated in *Childcare and Early Years* (2002, 12: 15): '"Central to the model is the development of inclusive provision rather than simply the creation of token places." Your policies and procedures must start with a solid premise such as this.'

Raising awareness

Some settings will need to take small steps in changing how they operate to be an inclusive service. Creating time to plan and reflect on the necessary tasks will be important. Raising everyone's awareness about these 'steps' will also need some planning, as managers will want to 'take the team with them', to make the changes happen.

A way of circulating the information on any of the policies of the setting is to have a standard agreement as part of the application to use the service. This will only work if the statement of policy has been included in any leaflet or shown in a booklet for the parents/carers or young people to see. It can be as simple as having the sentence, 'I have read the policies of the service and agree to abide by them. Signed . . . Date . . .'

Other ways of raising awareness include:

- having essential points displayed. Some will automatically be included in the 'ground rules' of the service, which the children could be part of by making suggestions;

- reviewing the activities and play opportunities offered (see Chapter 10). Ask directly where certain activities encourage stereotyping, sexism or other barriers for some children and explore this with the team. This could be done verbally or by a questionnaire;

- holding a discussion with the team on the policies and how they are implemented in the service – what do they find difficult to deal with personally?;

- designing or buying in board games on inclusion and equality of opportunities to encourage discussions and learning appropriate to children's level of development;

- deciding on whether to celebrate all major religious festivals. Some settings do, others have decided not to celebrate any. Both approaches may be perfectly valid for the children of your setting – ask them where possible;

- displaying *The New Charter for Children's Play* (Children's Play Council 1999).

Other methods may include news-sheets/newsletters; type of children's work on display, e.g. dragon masks for Chinese New Year; using an evaluation process to highlight sections of any policy or practice that is being phased out or in.

'The basic principles of inclusive management which underpin all the leader's work should be to value and involve each person with whom he or she works' (PIP Guidelines Series 1, 2002).

Language and terminology

Prejudice and discrimination will still go on despite the law and despite written policies if people are not made aware of their own behaviour or language and challenged about this when necessary.

Some expressions have changed to eliminate discrimination as much as possible; for example the term 'handicapped' to describe a person with a disability. This is outmoded and, in fact, incorrect terminology. It was a word invented during the late Victorian period to mean 'cap in hand', because some people with a disability relied on charity from others for their survival (holding out a cap for the money to be put into). The word spastic was commonly used for people with cerebral palsy; the charity Scope was at one time called the Spastics Society, but fortunately this has also changed.

Managers will need to review their own understanding of common definitions and use of phrases, as well as the teams and the children. We have included some definitions in the Glossary but two that are vital to the development of effective practice and sound policies are:

Inclusive practice: actively seeking ways of including children, whatever their background, culture, race, gender, sexual orientation, language or abilities, in a play/learning setting and encouraging their all-round development and understanding of themselves and others.

Discrimination: placing a person or a group of people at a disadvantage due to prejudice or stereotyping. Discrimination can be direct or indirect. Direct is open, e.g. refusing a disabled child access to your service because it would result in more work. Indirect discrimination is hidden, e.g. asking only the girls to help clear away the plates and mugs.

As you can see, these are opposites. One allows for the development of understanding, acceptance and learning; the other fosters a range of consequences such as the denial of self-worth, a feeling of non-identity, bullying, and in some cases war, of course.

If managers do not understand some of the basic terminology they cannot explain it to others, or break patterns that are based on misunderstanding, fear and ignorance. It is common to believe that people who show prejudices openly are ignorant, however that is not necessarily the case. A manager's role is to oversee the well-being of *every* child at the setting and prevent other adults, or children, showing their prejudices. Tolerance is the only professional stance acceptable when working with children and their parents. Through increased awareness and understanding of what others may find offensive in terminology and phrasing, we can be more sensitive to the other person's position.

Interactions and interventions

From an early age children learn there are differences in gender, language, clothes, colour, food, to name but a few. Their behaviour and attitude is influenced by the way they have caught, or been taught about, the diversity of others. Their thinking on how to treat other people and, indeed, how they see themselves in relation to others will be reflected in that understanding of the world.

It is vital that all adults are aware of their role with regard to countering discrimination and are given support in doing this. The team should have the opportunity to discuss a diverse range of methods to assist in dealing with discrimination that arises in the setting. This will not only help support them but also explore what attitudes prevail at the setting.

Interactions

All teams should be informed of the range of policies and procedures that they are working to in the setting during their induction. In addition all teams, including any volunteers, should attend training on a number of issues and subjects that are relevant to their work with children and young people, including what inclusive practice is. A manager would be wise to make sure that both of these things happen.

As mentioned before, adults and children alike may have to learn about other people's traditions, cultures, beliefs, abilities and needs, depending on their own background and experiences. Informing the children and their families of the setting's policies on anti-discrimination is always necessary.

Children and adults must be informed clearly that the following cannot be tolerated in any way at the setting:

- racism
- sexism
- homophobia
- harassment
- discrimination on ability.

Children must get the clear impression from **all** the team and manager/s that discrimination will be dealt with, whether intentional or not.

It will help if the team act cohesively and consistently in how they deal with discrimination. Inclusive activities can be planned and organised with the help of families of the children as well as the team. A genuine approach to this will mean there is no element of tokenism.

Use of posters in different languages (the most common one is the 'Welcome' poster in 12 different languages commonly spoken in the UK) and ones showing athletes with disabilities will also give a constant, visual reminder that differences are good, not a way of defining any one person as being 'less' than another.

Interventions: responding to inappropriate remarks or behaviour

An inappropriate remark can be devastating to the victim. The need to respond explicitly to both the victim and the addresser can be met in a range of ways. Talking openly with the children (if the remark was made by a child), by using a questioning tone and open gestures rather than an angry telling off with a pointing finger, can deal with the immediate effects if the victim is emotionally calm. For example, 'Why do you think it is not helpful/kind/accurate to say . . .?' 'What do you think this person is feeling?' Depending on the age of the children, a private one-to-one chat with the child who made the remark could also be necessary. However always check that the victim is all right and receives attention first. Support for them will highlight that the remark or action was not acceptable.

Managers need to develop the confidence to deal with an adult who makes a remark that is inappropriate. Holding an open discussion at a team meeting about adults' use of language would highlight the issue but is not always enough. In addition there may be a need to discuss on a private basis that team member's actions; this has the added benefit of helping them feel they have increased their understanding of discrimination rather than been picked on.

The severity of the remark or behaviour would determine what action the manager and/or team would need to take. If a child constantly uses phrases, words, or actions against another child or a member of the team and it is obvious that the child holds views that are discriminatory, a discussion alone would not be sufficient. Challenging and reviewing their behaviour would be more suitable.

Appropriate challenges A racist remark or one that discriminates against a person's ability needs to be challenged openly and in front of other children.

An appropriate challenge does not involve the adult losing their temper or raising their voice. It is one that stops the flow of conversation and points out that the remark is inaccurate, inappropriate, not acceptable. It may involve stopping the activity altogether to discuss why. Pointing out it is against the rules of the site is ineffectual and should only ever come as a last point. The addresser should be encouraged to apologise but the main aim of the challenge is to emphasise that racism and other prejudices are not acceptable and point out why they are not. The challenge is to stop the 'scene' and deal with the incident.

Children need to see challenges being made by the team because it reinforces the point that policies are there to protect *everyone*. More importantly it makes the setting a 'safe' place to be, proving that adults can be trusted to follow through the procedures and support every child.

CASE STUDY

Tomás, manager of the after-school club, is sharing a table at snack time with Joseph, who is from East Africa and has not been in England very long. He notices that Joseph eats with his hands and not the knife and fork. One of the boys sitting at the table laughs at him and calls him a baby for not being able to use the cutlery. Tomás intervenes by asking the boy to stop laughing and explaining that people from different countries have other ways of eating. He asks the boy who laughed what food he eats with his fingers, opening up the discussion to involve other things, and then asks Joseph what he has found different.

Tomás challenged the behaviour of the boy who laughed and called Joseph a baby in a gentle way that involved all of them learning and understanding a little more about cultural differences and practices.

Some do's and don'ts when responding to inappropriate remarks

DON'T

- Ignore any discriminatory remark even if it was 'meant' as a joke; it implies it is 'OK' here to say things like that.

- Shout or get angry.

- Threaten exclusion or sacking if the policies of the setting do not include this.

- Fail to monitor and review because of lack of time or resources.

- Give someone a book and tell them to read that instead of talking to them directly.

- Ignore the victim/s.

- Call the perpetrator names in retaliation.

- Deal with it in private behind closed doors – this gives mixed messages to the children and to other team members – *however* it may be necessary as the second stage of dealing with the incident.

DO

- Read up on policies and good practice.

- Attend training or discussion groups on inclusive practice.

- Bring up issues of dealing with discrimination in team meetings.

- Have an open mind but be prepared to say 'that is not acceptable'.

- Look for ways that support the team in good practice with regard to anti-discrimination, e.g. get a speaker or parent to discuss cultural issues at a team meeting.

- Look at your own personal language and attitudes.

- Review and monitor policies and make changes if necessary.

- Use the support of a local SENCO (Special Educational Needs Co-ordinator). [As part of the current government's initiative to implement the National

Childcare Strategy most local authorities or Early Years Development and Childcare Partnerships have someone whose role it is to support settings with children who have additional needs.]

CASE STUDY

Bella is one of the volunteers at a local playgroup. A mother brings her three-year-old child who has cerebral palsy. Bella says to the mother, 'I am afraid we have very little equipment for crippled children here.' Nur, the manager, hears this and comes over to the mother and Bella, saying to Bella, 'The child is not a cripple, Bella; she has a physical impairment, that's all. We can adapt lots of equipment if we think about it.' Nur talks to Bella after the playgroup has finished; she asks Bella to sit down opposite her and explains to her that words and phrases can really cause offence, even if unintentional. Nur asks Bella to reflect on her use of the word 'cripple' and points out why it is out of date and inappropriate. Bella is defensive and remarks that she has always used that word and grew up with it. Nur reminds her that the playgroup wishes to remain inclusive to all children and how important a resource it has been for local parents and children, and for that child in particular in helping her develop to her full potential. Bella agrees to watch her language; in addition Nur mentions a few training courses that might help Bella.

Putting it into practice

- Start by reflecting on your own approach and attitudes.

- Be aware of your own language and behaviour to watch out for hidden prejudices.

- Think about ways of acknowledging cultural diversity within the setting – even if you have no young people from other cultures.

- Discuss areas of discrimination at team meetings to improve skills and knowledge. Make sure you and the team do not differentiate between boys and girls according to stereotypes of gender, e.g. having only a group of girls do a cookery activity.

- Have clearly written policies on inclusion showing how the setting will deal with discrimination.

- Have a mixture of equipment and books that all children, whatever their abilities, can access.

- Look into training some of the team in special skills so your centre can be all-inclusive, e.g. learning sign language.

- When dealing with intentional discrimination, remain calm but firm; use eye contact when stating why you will not accept what that individual or group has done or said.

- Never leave discriminatory language or actions unchallenged.

- Get advice and support from others to develop your setting's inclusive practice.

CHAPTER 8

Time management

Being able to plan work and programmes of activities is an essential skill for managers in child-centred settings. Being able to plan and manage one's own time is just as important but we do not always feel that it is in our control. Some people early on in life acquire the personality traits that make time management easier for them, others need to develop the skills and master their own approaches to coping with numerous tasks and responsibilities as a manager.

Two points are true for all of us. One, we all need to practise managing our time effectively, and two, methods will change from job to job and from gathering experience of management. However, our basic approach and attitude to time and our own work may remain the same, especially if we have mastered some techniques that help us.

Essential skills for time management

- Exploring methods to manage your time more effectively

- Saying 'no' and reinforcing personal boundaries

- Knowing your time wasters

- Knowing how to prioritise tasks

- Distinguishing between important and urgent tasks

Why is time management important?

This may appear obvious to some managers and not to others. We believe that by developing the skills to manage your time you will be a more effective manager, i.e. you will have increased confidence, less stress, more time to think. This in turn can make the job easier and more satisfying, with the spin-offs being increased enthusiasm and more involvement with the people whom the child-centred setting is there for. By having good systems of working, a manager can analyse work and see where future problems might arise and therefore be prepared.

We all have different attitudes to time and to the personal management of time. Some of these attitudes are adopted by us from our childhood, or from our cultural experiences. Others are habits developed by us to cope with working life but, in fact, may not help us to be an effective manager. The issues and tasks arising from our responsibilities as managers in this sector have the largest impact on our planning and management of time.

Robert Heller and Tim Hindle (1998) suggest that the ideal allocation of time for managers should be as follows:

> 60% of time on planning and development
> 25% of time on projects
> 15% of time on routine tasks.

In actual fact, for most of us it is very different, of course! It is more like

> 60% of time spent on routine tasks
> 25% of time on projects
> 15% of time on planning and development.

For example:

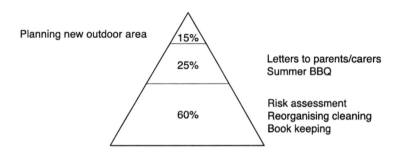

Figure 8.1 *Time management*

Many managers of child-centred settings are also part of the team working with the children, so would probably laugh at the idea of trying to reorganise their time to have 60 per cent of time on developing projects. However, by taking some time to look at our own working patterns, reorganising, planning or simply reinforcing boundaries and, of course, by being honest with ourselves, we may find we can get a little closer to the 'ideal' of 60 per cent than we had first thought.

Developing your own skills

There is no one method or set of rules that works better than another. We need to develop ways according to our priorities and the responsibilities of the job we are currently doing. The team you work with may include more than your immediate colleagues; for instance, management committee members, Childcare Development Advisers and, of course, parents. All these people and services can have an impact on your working day and therefore on when and how you get your work done and manage your own tasks and responsibilities.

The Three-Minute Decision

If a task, or series of tasks, will only take three minutes each, by opting to do them all first you clear a lot of work (e.g. paying invoices, making a call to a delivery firm, confirming a meeting). You can then put the rest of the time to good use.

Tried and tested methods for time management

For all methods your starting point is **your attitude** to time management. Do you want to change the way you are managing your time? Are you getting the job done the way you would ideally like to? How much time do you have to enjoy the work you do? Being aware of your own approach to time management, looking for ways that you can make improvements, is a useful exercise for all of us.

There are always demands that compete and on an average day time is in fact 'wasted' by a series of routine tasks being interrupted and not completed. By analysing how we use our time we can see where we need to make adjustments and develop approaches that make effective use of the time we have.

In a child-centred setting much of the management is based around routines and helping the team and volunteers meet the needs of the children. It may be that a realistic analysis of your workload for your particular setting would show you need to spend a large percentage of your time on routine tasks. But remember to look carefully at your reasons for this; ask yourself some questions such as these:

1   Are there patterns or habits that could be changed?

2   Are you delegating enough?

3   Is someone not pulling their weight?

4   Do you need more staff in the team or volunteers?

5   Are you putting the difficult tasks aside?

6   Are you saying 'no' enough?

Method one

- Look at the various aspects of your role as manager of a child-centred setting; a job description, if you have one, will help with this. Make a list of daily tasks.

- Estimate how much time you spend on each of the tasks using half-hourly or hourly measurements. Add up the time spent on tasks. Is your total more than the hours you have in a day?

- Beside each of the tasks and time spent write what time you *would like* to spend on it. Add this up and compare it with the actual time spent.

- Write a list of time wasters that frequently stand in the way of you achieving your plan for the day. This list of questions may help you:

1   Am I doing anybody else's work?

2   Am I doing something that a member of the team could do?

3   Do some tasks take longer than I thought they would?

4   Do I attend too many meetings?

5   Am I saying 'yes' when I should say 'no'?

6   Am I not making my needs clear?

7   Have I allowed myself some thinking and planning time?

8   Have I any patterns of work I am unhappy about?

- Using the breakdown of 'ideal' and 'actual' time used above, how would you break your day down? Are you spending more time on one group of tasks than you need to or would like to?

- Draw up a list of tasks that could be routine and must be done each day, a list of tasks that you would like to do and a list that could be delegated to another member of the team. Put this somewhere you can refer to it regularly during the day, such as a wall chart, a day book, or a flipchart in the corner of your room.

- Cross off tasks when you have done them – it makes you feel a lot better!

Method two

- As for method one, call to mind all your tasks and write a list at random without thinking too much.

- Draw up a daily or weekly sheet with five main areas under these headings:

    Priorities   Routine tasks   Phone calls   Meetings   Carry forward

Call it something such as My Daily/Weekly Action Plan or Tasks Sheet and keep it in a folder so you can track your action points over a period of time. Evaluation and review are important aspects of developing effective time management skills.

- Put items from your list in the relevant columns.

- By each item you put on the sheet put a time period, e.g. 1.00–1.30 pm. This way you can look to see if certain tasks are taking longer and ask yourself why. A lack of staff could be one reason but that is temporary. What you are looking for are areas you can change, habits that detract from completing tasks and hold you up from doing the planning and development side of your work. Look at 'Knowing your time wasters' below to see if you recognise any of the common ones.

- When you know what distracts you and what takes up some of your time unnecessarily then you can start to build in 'defences' and alter your pattern of work and, therefore, become efficient in managing your time most of the day.

Some people use large sheets of paper from flip charts to do this, others have it on their computers or in a daily work book – do what works for you, try various ways until you are happy.

How we use time during our average working day becomes habitual. In some organisations, for instance, working long hours is equated with working hard. Most of us realise that this is not the case. Organisational culture can have a deep impact on use of time and how people relate to each other, regardless of whether they are willing to take on responsibilities. In addition to working on your own habits, think about what organisational habits have developed for others in the team; 'making an initial investment of time to rethink and improve' (Heller and Hindle 1998) and changing your own way of working will have an impact on theirs.

Saying 'no' and reinforcing boundaries

An important part of managing your own workload is setting boundaries for others to adhere to – unless there is an emergency. Managers who are constantly interrupted by their team for decisions or information will never feel that they can get any substantial task completed.

Saying 'no' does not mean you are an authoritarian manager who is not available to support the team and/or children. It does mean that you have the right to allocate certain working time to the management tasks that you have given priority to and that need your full attention. If you have allocated time in the week or day to tackle a task that requires you to concentrate and focus it is best not to accept any phone calls, visitors or disturbances. A simple explanation to all the team that this is what you are going to do normally suffices, but occasionally you will have to be assertive and repeat what it is you need. Assertion theory calls this the 'Stuck Record'. State very clearly what you need; do not use phrases such as 'I am afraid . . .' After all, you as manager will need time to work on issues for the centre.

It will be difficult if you do not have an office area; try to form a screen around you with other equipment or, if in a school, ask to use another room.

Voicing your needs can be done in a variety of ways: putting up a jokey sign, such as 'Quiet, genius at work'; mentioning in supervision and team meetings that you are going to have to work on your own with no disturbances and saying when and for how long; closing your office door and diverting calls or putting the phone on the answer machine or placing the phone outside of your office so others can answer it. Asking the management committee to find the funds for staff cover while you work at home on a task may be another option.

> **CASE STUDY**
>
> Geraldine, as manager of a large crèche, wanted to work on a new funding application form that required plans for extending the staff and space. She talked about her ideas for this at a team meeting and said to all the staff that she needed time to prepare the application and, therefore, would be in the kitchen (as she did not have an office) from 10.30 to 12.30 on the following Monday. She then said she would require the team to take all calls or visitors' queries unless there was an emergency. She emphasised that she would not open the door to any knock or answer any query; she also explained what she believed was an emergency that she could be disturbed for. On the Monday she reminded all staff and put a notice on the door to the kitchen. She made sure that she spent the two hours fruitfully and reappeared at 12.30 p.m. as she had stated she would.

A final point: do be mindful of members of your team whose cultural experiences or perceptions of time are different from yours. Clear explanations with patient reminding from time to time will show by example how you wish to operate.

Knowing your time wasters

The usual time wasters that managers have noted include:

- delays in traffic/public transport
- phone calls upon arrival, such as parents who have forgotten to give information
- non-delivery of essential items, such as the food for snack time
- chatting over coffee/tea
- the team wanting advice, feedback, decisions while the manager is doing something else
- the team arriving late, so the manager does tasks
- parents/carers visiting unexpectedly and wanting to talk about their child
- someone forgetting to finish a task so the manager does it
- inessential meetings, such as the treasurer wanting to check figures given already
- meetings dragging on beyond the time allocated
- cleaners not doing their job
- long phone calls

- broken or old equipment

- no answerphone.

Some of the reasons why these become time wasters:

- no time to plan or prioritise tasks

- untidy desks or inadequate work space

- previous patterns adopted by new manager

- misunderstanding of job roles and responsibilities

- lack of equipment to support you

- miscommunication.

How to prioritise tasks

Ask yourself, when writing your list of routine tasks and priorities, how important they are; list them A, B, C or 1, 2, 3. A tasks are ones that you should try to complete every day, or at least a few of them; B tasks are the ones that you spend most of your time doing, so are routine ones; and C tasks are those that you can do perhaps at the end of the day, or maybe they can be delegated, again usually routine tasks.

Think about how you rate something as being a 'priority'. Is it, for instance, because your management committee has asked for it? Is it to do with your legal obligations? Is it to make life easier for others? Is there a deadline, as for funding applications?

All this information needs to be considered when putting a task down as being a priority. Remember also that priorities may change from day to day because of new information, emergencies that need to be dealt with and other events.

Evaluate your priorities as you go through the day, moving them accordingly. Occasionally you will have a conflict of priorities with your team or management committee or have many more listed in a priority plan than you can actually deal with. The following list may help if you find yourself in that situation:

1   Try to do at least one of your 'absolutely essential' tasks each day and at least two of the tasks that need to be done, in addition to any routine tasks.

2   If one of the tasks is boring, complicated, or generally not easy to do, tackle it first thing in the morning. It will make the day go better and give you a clearer mind to get on with other planned action points. THIS REALLY WORKS.

3   Allocate a time in the day when you will deal with all mail, phone calls and/or visitors; if need be, make this a quiet time and shut your door. Don't forget to tell others that you are doing this and why. Emergencies are an acceptable interruption!

4   If some priority tasks cannot yet be done because you are waiting for information or further details, put a note to yourself in a diary or on an action plan to chase it up so you can meet your deadline. If others need to know this, inform them as soon as possible.

5   When thinking about a long-term plan and the year ahead, remember what cycles your work has; e.g. if your playgroup or after-school club closes during the holidays, your list of long-term action points will need to take this into consideration. Those that are a priority will have to be completed in the time cycle that you work in. Towards the end of a school term the team are generally tired and not able to muster very much enthusiasm for changes; bear that in mind when planning work loads.

6   Remember to explain to others you are working with why a task may not be completed in time.

Despite the old adage 'Don't put off till tomorrow that which can be done today', we often do not have a choice in the matter; priorities will get moved.

Gentle but firm reminders will often need to be made. A notice on your door, if you have an office, is one way.

IMPORTANT: we all have different ideas about what an emergency is, so state what you consider this to be. Many managers would baulk at not being available for others at any time but it is a common time waster. If you are happy with your current arrangement, then that's fine.

CASE STUDY

Frankie manages an adventure playground; she has a list of daily routine tasks. In addition, she has been working on her NVQ Level 3 in Playwork and she has two units to finish by the end of the month to meet the deadline. There was an emergency yesterday, one of the team is off on First Aid training this week and Frankie will need to deal with two young people accused of bullying if they come to the centre today. Frankie draws up a list of all her tasks for this afternoon and what else she needs to do during the week. Her NVQ work is important and she decides to prioritise that for the afternoon. Next she puts the emergency from yesterday at the top of her list, as she can write the report and letters within 30 minutes. She then decides to delegate dealing with the two accused of bullying to the senior playworker. She makes a note to talk to him as soon as he comes in and immediately gets out the file. She also makes a note to herself about dealing with bullying and accusations of this for the following week's team meeting, which reminds her she has not typed up the notes from the previous one yet. She then looks again at her list, puts a time by everything and decides to do the minutes first, then the NVQ work, as the minutes will be useful evidence for her qualification, then she will do all routine tasks that take longer than three minutes.

> This way Frankie goes through her list – not ignoring the routine tasks but reorganising what she has to do first, then second, and so on. She can delegate a task and this frees up her time. She now has a clear idea of what she can get completed in the time she has.

Urgent or important?

Tasks listed in your daily/weekly plan can be arranged according to their urgency or importance. Urgent tasks are those that need your attention or can be delegated straight away to be carried out within an immediate time frame. They will have a major impact on the setting in some way, such as getting food supplies in for snack time. Important tasks are those that either need action but not straight away, or need several different points to be completed at different stages, e.g. ordering new stock or equipment before the end of term or before the summer playscheme begins. Being able to differentiate between the two will help you schedule your action plan accordingly and, of course, re-prioritise your list of tasks when necessary.

Putting it into practice

- Planning your day and your week is *never* a waste of time. MAKE time to do it.

- Dealing with a difficult task, or part of it, straight away makes you feel better and leaves you thinking more clearly.

- Keep a diary or calendar with meetings, appointments, etc., visible. Some people who do not have an office space use electronic methods; others use pen and paper in a special pocket notebook.

- Every so often, monitor time needed for completing tasks against your plan.

- Ask more about the meeting you are being asked to attend: do you really need to go? Think about what you and your service will get from the meeting. Can a phone call or a letter do it?

- Ask parents to make an appointment to see you, unless they have an emergency.

- Allocate a time each day or each week when you can attend to the tasks you need to get down to without interruptions.

- If you find you have too many 'Absolutely essential' tasks then you will need to delegate some of your routine or 'Better done today' tasks to others.

- Alter priorities when need be – don't keep rigidly to your plan.

- Remember if you have set yourself a deadline it is to help you, not to cause more stress. Give yourself a treat when you meet a deadline.

- Practise skills in time management, see where you can improve – don't give up!

CHAPTER 9

Building a team

Managing teams is a key part of the role and duties of a manager, however big or small the team is. In some cases the childcare team is only two people, which will require a different approach and set of skills from the ones we are looking at in this book. For this chapter, we consider a team to be at least three people, one of whom may be the manager.

Although you cannot change a person's personality you will need to manage personalities as part of building a team. One of the main skills of doing this is to understand you cannot change anyone, they can only change themselves. However those who do not alter their attitude or approach when asked may have need of further training and supervision. We suggest that the team has a clear set of procedures of working with the manager and others in the setting.

The manager's role in building a team is an ongoing one. Managers need to bring together a group of individuals that as a 'whole' can work together, balancing the individual skills and qualities with the job in hand. Your most important asset is the people working for you, so how well they work together has a huge impact on the atmosphere of the setting. Getting this right is part of the manager's job.

Essential skills for team building

- Understanding basic theory on how team traits and dynamics impact on teams

- Recognising your leadership style

- Identifying individual and team strengths and weaknesses

- Developing the team

- Recognising factors of motivation and demotivation for individuals

Why is team development important?

There are two ways of looking at the manager's position of leading the team. Some theorists would advise a manager to think of themselves as a team servant, being part of the team and not just managing it, balancing the roles of the individual staff members, the team as a whole and the task. Other theorists believe the manager is not part of the team but directing and supporting the team as a leader, leading from the front, monitoring aspects of the work, offering encouragement and vision, getting the job done. This theory has many advantages, especially for child-centred settings, e.g. someone is always keeping an eye on the way ahead while the team are busy being with the children.

In addition to building and motivating the team, the manager may have a role as a referee dealing with team conflicts and clashes of personality. How you deal with this will depend on your own level of confidence and experience. (See Chapter 1.)

Developing your own skills

Understanding basic theory on team traits and dynamics

Team building requires constant observation and supervision, which can be carried out in a number of ways and does not mean in any way that the team cannot be trusted or that the manager has to be a 'fly on the wall'. What we mean is that the dynamics of a team can change and will change and a manager is wise to be aware of this, keeping an 'eye out' for differences that might have an impact on working relationships, the tasks being carried out and the general well-being of all the team.

No matter how small or large your staff team is, there are a number of roles that people play and responsibilities that could be allocated to each member according to skills, experience and personality. As you will know, personalities have a major impact on a team's dynamics. There are two theories regarding this that we think could help you and which we outline in brief below. If you are attracted by either of these we have given suggestions for further reading in the Bibliography at the end of the book.

The team traits theory

The best known theorist on team roles, whose work has been used in all kinds of management training and development, is Dr Meredith Belbin. He studied team behaviour and structure for over 25 years and in this research identified nine key roles that impact on teams working together. He recognised that we as individuals have a natural tendency to assume particular roles, called traits, according to our personality, our way of thinking and behaving. His research on the individual traits makes interesting reading as he indicates the advantages and disadvantages of each. The nine roles/traits are Completer, Coordinator, Implementer, Monitor/evaluator, Plant, Resource investigator, Shaper, Specialist, and Team worker. You can read more about these individual traits in several books on management and team building, including Dr Belbin's.

Dynamics of team development

Many factors play a part in the dynamics of a team and these factors change all the time. What we mean by dynamics is the energy, processes and methods of working together that a group of people use to get on with the job and to get on with each other.

The other theorist that you may find useful is B. W. Tuckman, who studied and researched the way groups of people develop together. He analysed different stages of development and labelled each stage according to what is going on:

FORMING – There is not yet a team but a group of individuals who are polite, cautious, and uncertain of their role and purpose and the direction of the team.

STORMING – Personal agendas are revealed, sometimes resulting in challenges to responsibilities and roles; people try to get to know what the team needs to do and who will do it.

NORMING – The team establishes ways of working, sets patterns of working practice and levels of commitment, and builds trust.

PERFORMING – Getting on with the job, with sharing and supportive teamwork, the team is productive and able to meet objectives.

When the team is new or if a new member has joined the team, a manager's role is to support the *forming* stage. This may mean more 'hands on', more direction and supervision, friendly checking up on the situation and observation. When the team is at the next stage, *storming*, there can be confusion and distrust that cause conflicts in the team. Here a manager's role is to mediate, remain open-minded and consistent in approach to all members of the team and find a solution with the team by being rational, producing facts if necessary. At the *norming* stage the team needs a manager to be the organiser and motivator to keep the team's momentum. At the final stage of *performing*, the manager is a facilitator for new ideas, problem solving, personal and professional development and setting new goals or targets with the team, keeping them focused on achieving the vision.

Recognising your leadership style

The main function of a manager is to achieve the aims and objectives of the setting. How you are as a manager will be reflected in how successful you are in developing and building your team and leading the team in carrying out their tasks to provide a service to children. There are theories on styles of leadership, such as autocratic and democratic, analysed and developed by John Adair (2002). Modern views of leadership include the approaches of managers being akin to coaching, supervising, motivating, etc.

We believe it is far more important to concentrate on being an assertive leader and develop skills and practices that help you manage the team than to worry about which style of leader you should be in any given situation. We suggest that you look at your communication skills, your understanding of how you are received, if and how you are restricting your team. People respond to the atmosphere in child-centred settings, how the team works together and gets along; how the manager 'manages' will be a major contributory factor to this.

Identifying your team's strengths and weaknesses

A manager could start by taking a look at their team as a whole:

- What are the team's strengths and weaknesses?

- How does each member of the team contribute to these?

By capitalising on strengths you can develop skills, enthusiasm and team spirit. If you have an enthusiastic and motivated team working with you, the atmosphere is good, the job becomes more rewarding and people enjoy coming to work. It can also help cut down on staff illness. New ideas are generated because people feel they are heard and valued and the beneficiaries of all this are, of course, the children you are providing a service to.

Reflect on your own team for a moment:

- Do all your team understand their roles and responsibilities? This is different from just knowing the tasks and doing them.

- What have you done as a manager that would help individual team members get the full picture of what the team is there to do?

- Does your team have the opportunity for regular feedback?

- Is this feedback given freely and openly or are some people holding back information and experience?

- Does your team communicate openly and supportively with each other?

- Are they flexible to change?

- Who and what has influence on the team? For example, does the day-to-day physical environment influence the team?

Developing the team

The first step in building an effective team is to look at the people you have working with you. The right skills and knowledge are a desirable component but by no means an essential one, as staff can develop these while they work as long as the atmosphere in the setting is conducive to on-the-job learning. What you do need are people who want to be there because they enjoy being with children and feel they have something to offer and to learn. They are the most important asset you have.

Here are some methods and approaches for building an effective team:

- Match tasks to team roles until skills develop and then offer a chance to change.

- Hold regular team meetings and send the agenda round a week before for comments.

- Ask if staff want to have a 'roving' chair at meetings, so everyone gets a chance to chair and develop skills.

- Train the team together.

- Hold individual supervision sessions weekly or fortnightly.

- Always be fair.

- Keep the team informed of new developments and changes as they happen.

- Treat everyone as part of the team, including the person who 'just does the snacks' or 'just does the escorting'.

- Think about improvements to the working environment that would help, such as painting the staff room or having a coffee machine.

- Deal with any brewing issues that may quickly cause conflict.

- Set clear, achievable targets.

Other suggestions

Socialising. Managers can support the working dynamics of a team by socialising when possible with them to learn more about the individuals they work with. Be mindful of equal opportunity issues here, such as not suggesting meeting in a pub or wine bar if members of the team do not drink alcohol or for religious reasons cannot enter a venue that sells it.

Developing people. Highlight interesting and relevant training opportunities: show appreciation of the skills and knowledge staff have; actively show you will listen to new ideas, concerns or suggestions and encourage team members to support each other; ask for some tasks to be done in pairs or small groups, depending on the size of the team.

New team members. When recruiting new members to the team, include existing staff in making decisions about new job roles and the interviewees; this can also help the team accept a new person more quickly. This may not always be possible in child-centred settings but if the candidates for the job are shown around and meet some of the team you will be making a good impression on the new person, helping them get a picture of where they will be working and with whom, as well as allowing existing staff to be involved. (This, of course, does not happen very often with holiday playschemes where individuals are selected and interviewed before the scheme starts and there are usually many new faces joining the team each year.) Keeping an eye on the new person for the next month or two will also help.

Ground rules of working together. Drawing up a code of practice that enables your team to work together is a good tool in effective team building. Emphasising points such as actively listening, respecting different opinions, trying out others' ideas, and not cutting across someone else when they are speaking, will help the team not only hold an effective meeting but also work amiably alongside each other.

As manager you may have to remind individuals what the team has agreed upon or suggest that some points be added or taken away. Confidentiality is a point that is often overlooked when teams design a code to operate by, but it is an important issue that needs to be discussed in teams.

Team meetings. These are an important opportunity for a manager to receive feed-back, keep staff informed, get an update on how things are going, and explore ideas. However, not all team members need be at every meeting, depending on the agenda and aim of the meeting.

The problem that most managers of settings in childcare have is finding the right time and location for these meetings. It may be that you have to be creative and book some space in the local café or coffee shop to hold the meeting. This may entail people working in their own time and you need to decide whether this is appropriate. Can you offer recompense in some way, such as leave in lieu, or payment?

You will have in your team some staff members who are vocal and some who are not. Do not let those who are not get swamped or ignored in the process. Their views and experiences are just as important and they may require your assistance in getting them heard.

Be prepared for the meeting. Circulate a draft agenda to all attending, and ask for comments and suggestions. If you have anyone coming from outside the setting to the meeting, be sure to state this in the agenda. Remember we often need a change of communication medium at team meetings – which are predominantly talk – to take in additional information. Visual diagrams, photos, videos if applicable, etc. all add to keeping up the learning and the momentum of the meeting. Remind staff the night before that the meeting is going ahead and at what time.

It is important that you as manager do the following:

- Keep to the time and encourage others to do so.

- Welcome anyone new to the team.

- Ask for someone to take notes.

- Discuss each item on the agenda and ensure that all have an opportunity to speak.

- Do not let meetings drag on over the time allocated, especially if staff have given up their own time to attend.

> **CASE STUDY**
>
> Joan had been coordinating the Playing in the Sun holiday scheme for the local council for many years. This year she needed a much bigger team and realised that she would need regular team meetings. To start with, once a week she and the team went to the local café after work and discussed the week so far and what they wanted for the next week. Joan asked for a different person to take the notes of the meeting and chair it every time. They did this in alphabetical order by first name. In addition they met every morning for 15 minutes, before the children arrived, to discuss the day and individual children and for Joan to give out information. She was strict with times, allowing only three minutes per person and making sure everyone was included.

Motivational and demotivational factors

It is generally understood that most people will share some motivational factors regarding work, added to which will be individual reasons for work and personal aims. Kenneth Blanchard (1994) says of motivation, 'Most people are enthusiastic beginners . . . I think people only lose their commitment when they realise that good performance does not make a difference.' Managers can maintain motivation of staff if they understand that the common factors for all of us hinge very often on their actions and behaviour.

Common factors that motivate people include money, job satisfaction, status, recognition, security, responsibility, and meeting a need within the community. One or two of these factors have little relevance to work in the childcare sector as pay is not high and security cannot be guaranteed. However, a manager will need to bear in mind that individuals do want recognition but not all want responsibility. People in general want to be paid on time and for the work they do and feel that their work is worthwhile even if what they do is not fully understood by the wider community.

Individual motivation for working comes from:

- goals that at the same time are achievable and teach new skills or understanding

- promotion or career opportunities

- being able to learn something new regularly

- being part of a responsive and effective team

- being needed

- using personal skills and knowledge

- having a regular job with hours that suit personal commitments

- doing something different every day.

CASE STUDY

Hafiz had just taken over a small nursery with five staff, two of whom had been at the setting for six years. He realised that there was no meeting area for the staff, no regular system of appraisal and very little motivation in the team. He worked out a rota of weekly supervision with each member of the team and held team meetings once every three weeks. He then allocated part of the large entrance area as a staff meeting place and placed screens to divide the area off, with comfortable chairs for the staff. Another member of staff felt motivated enough to bring in a few posters to put up and they all helped in making a notice board for their meeting area. Through the supervision sessions Hafiz was able to check that people understood their roles and responsibilities and that they knew they were able to attend training courses relevant to their work, and he gave them all an area of responsibility in the nursery within their own capacity and interest.

Things that lead to people feeling demotivated

Some demotivating factors will not be remedied overnight. For instance, personality clashes do occur; a manager can only deal with this as well as time and environment allow. A solution could be to suggest that if they, as individuals, can come to no accommodating solution they should work separately at the setting. Other elements in the demotivational cycle include:

- An individual's lack of understanding about their role in the team
- No induction into the job and the team, resulting in dissatisfaction and not knowing what they are there to do
- No meetings to allow concerns and issues to be raised
- Lack of commitment by one or more members of the team
- Workload too demanding, long hours
- Unreliability
- Lack of responsibility
- Lack of recognition for work done
- Not being involved in major decisions that affect them
- The manager being unfair – saying one thing and doing another
- The manager not acting on staff members' concerns.

By showing staff how their job fits into the overall vision of the setting and giving them opportunities to take part in the decision-making process, you will build on the effectiveness and overall success of the team. However, you will also need to deal with those issues that cause unrest in others, such as an individual team member being unreliable or showing no real commitment to the job. The other members of the team may consider it unfair if you do not attempt to find a solution to these issues, which, of course, may include dismissal.

Rewards

Rewards are a way of maintaining motivation. In childcare, a poorly paid sector on the whole, financial rewards are not always possible, so be creative!

Praise, if genuinely conveyed, is always welcome because we all like to be told we have done well. Team meetings are a good place for this but do not overdo it; some people cannot take praise very easily, so be sensitive to the individual/s.

Other suggestions are

- Thank you's, giving thanks by sending a card that others have signed as well

- Giving a gift such as a book, flowers, vouchers

- Promotion to another job, or the next level, or to other tasks that require more responsibility

- Allocating an extra day's holiday for commitment

- Arranging a treat for the whole team, such as a day out, lunch brought in for them, a night out together, or cream cakes for all!

- Free uniform.

Rewards must be fair; if one individual has obtained a reward so must another be able to. If it is for the whole team then the whole team must be able to benefit from it or enjoy it, e.g. do not give an ordinary birthday cake to someone suffering from coeliac disease who cannot eat gluten. In giving rewards make them public and personal. If giving a box of chocolates to each member because of their hard work during the year, do not leave them in the kitchen with their names on Post-its, give them personally to each member. Recognition is important to how we feel about ourselves; the reward is not just the chocolates, it is in your personal recognition of the individual. 'Many things affect confidence – even a few simple words' (Landsberg 2003: 23).

A final motivational factor

We all have common human needs, one of which is a sense of belonging, and another is **respect**. Much lip service is paid to the phrase 'showing respect'. We all think we know what each other means but do we? Our definition would include 'treat with consideration' (*Pocket Oxford English Dictionary* 1984). Added to this, we would say that respect means valuing others' opinions and support, not judging them, listening to their feedback and ideas, giving them time to speak, not talking over them, allowing for their individual needs, involving them in decisions that affect them, and so on. Trust and respect are not automatically given because someone has a title or position – it is a dynamic that has to be worked on. Being aware of this is the first step.

If you look at the team you work with, could you confidently say that you and others show all individuals respect? If not, this will add to a team working less effectively. We have a considerable role to play in showing how we value diversity in childcare, so we can help in the breaking down of many barriers that alienate people in our society today. If we are doing this openly with the children at our settings we need to reflect that in our relationships with each other.

Putting it into practice

- Be clear about what you are saying, expecting and can do.

- Ensure that you do not confuse your team by saying one thing then doing another.

- Look at how you are managing the team; you cannot expect to be trusted and respected just by having the title 'Manager'.

- There are pros and cons in most tasks, but not being recognised or rewarded for getting on with the job can breed dissatisfaction.

- People like to have control over their responsibilities; give them room to develop their own skills by allowing them this control.

- People need to feel included in a team and feel comfortable to work with others in the team; bring everyone together informally from time to time to learn more about each other and the work.

- Never leave a new member of staff to do their own introductions; always make them welcome and expect that they will be nervous and unsure at first and will need time to settle in.

- A set of ground rules or a code of working together that is not reinforced becomes a farce.

- Do not rush into dealing with all conflict issues; some resolve themselves. However, if an issue amongst the team is affecting the children at the setting and/or others in the team, raise this concern with those involved.

- Do not favour one member of the team, however well you get on with them.

- As manager you oversee how the team gets the job done; it is your responsibility to help individuals understand where their job fits into the overall picture and vision of the setting.

CHAPTER 10

Evaluation processes

Child-centred settings that regularly review their programme of activities – whether by a formal written review or by an informal gathering of data – will recognise that reviewing is a useful process which can often take place through regular, general discussions. A full evaluation of the setting is also effective.

Good practice and quality are not assured just because a setting has met all the needs of the children. Managers of settings need to think ahead, as well as looking at what has been happening before. Organising an evaluation process will enable a manager to do this competently. However well your setting is running, work from the assumption that every setting can be improved in some way.

Essential skills for organising an evaluation process

- Understanding the tasks of a manager

- Choosing a method

- Planning, collecting and analysing data

- Getting others involved

- Dealing with successes and failures

Why are evaluations important?

We believe the purpose of implementing an evaluation process is to look at the whole of the setting and the service provided to see if the aims and objectives set out in the beginning are being met. The prime aim is to judge whether value has been offered in the concept and operation of the setting, to take into consideration all the successes and the failures and to look for potential improvements. There are a number of tasks that the manager can carry out to make sure that the outcome is relevant and adds to the vision of the setting.

The evaluation process

The process of evaluation could be summarised as

Experience + Reflection = Learning

There are different theoretical ways of looking at the evaluation process; the circular model is one of the most popular:

Figure 10.1 *Evaluation process*

The experiences stage refers to the children's (or adults') experience of the service and the provision of different aspects of the setting.

Expressions of experiences refers to comments of the children and staff in a variety of ways according to their own interpretations of what they have felt, enjoyed, or not enjoyed about the various aspects of the setting and the programme.

Examining findings is where the team and/or manager look carefully at what has been said.

Exploring opportunities is the stage whereby new ideas and opportunities for change are looked at prior to making decisions for the future.

Executing changes is where the suggestions and comments made in the evaluation are put into practice.

The way the manager implements the process will have direct implications on the quality of the feedback. It is important not to look for 'scapegoats' or 'heroes/heroines' in the process; evaluations must remain open but focused on the aims of the evaluation.

Reviews and evaluations

Teams that hold regular informal reviews of the programme and setting will, in the main, be discussing current issues and points that need to be addressed; for example, what to do about the cleaning of the centre, what to do with a new child just registered who has different needs. If done openly and fairly, the review will help the manager keep on top of issues that arise regularly. However, an evaluation enables the manager to look at the *whole* programme, the service and the way it operates, investigating areas where quality can be improved.

A review would be held after an incident or to address an immediate need.

An evaluation would include how the service deals with incidents overall and how the service meets needs overall.

Developing your own skills

Most managers of child-centred settings look for ways to improve the service and setting in which they operate. To do this, managers need to know what is happening around them and how the children and team view what is on offer. The essential skills described in this chapter give managers a framework from which they can identify the necessary priorities and appropriate action to take when initiating a full evaluation programme.

The tasks of a manager

1 To set up the process and to ensure that it allows all who are connected with the setting to play a part in the evaluation – after all, the service is set up for the children!

2 To record and analyse the findings of the evaluation.

3 To draw up an action plan, based on the findings, and implement it.

Methods of evaluation

There is a wide variety of methods used in evaluation processes and some are used alongside each other.

Many settings would benefit from carrying out a **SWOT** analysis of the service they offer. SWOT is an acronym for

- **Strengths**
- **Weaknesses**
- **Opportunities**
- **Threats.**

A SWOT analysis can be done in two ways:

Formally: asking staff to complete, individually, a form that has each of these words on it and a space underneath for comments. A series of questions such as the ones below could be used.

- What do you think our strengths are?

- What do you think our weaknesses are?

- How can we build on our strengths?

- Are there any opportunities we have missed?

- What do you think the threats to our service are?

The benefit of this method would be that individuals could feed back their own thoughts and opinions and not feel swayed by others or keep quiet because others were more vocal. On the other hand, there would be no debate or discussion.

Informally: having a team meeting or a series of team meetings looking at each of the four areas of the SWOT process and recording the feedback on a flipchart or through note-taking. The benefit of this method would be to encourage everyone to discuss and debate and check which views are realistic and which are not, but then some staff may feel that they do not need to join in the discussion.

Evaluating these four areas with the staff team may assist you in devising the best way to carry out the evaluation and enable you to concentrate the questions on what you want to find out.

CASE STUDY

As manager of a playgroup, Clarise wanted to see if she could get more children and their parents/carers to attend. She decided that she would carry out an evaluation of the work of the playgroup and raised this idea at a team meeting with her three staff. There was some indecision as to what to ask in the evaluation, so Clarise decided that they needed to start with a SWOT analysis. She agreed to draw up some questions that they could discuss at the next team meeting. She drew up three questions covering each of the four areas and gave a set of them to each member of the team so they could think about it and prepare for the next meeting. Meanwhile she looked through her existing records to see if there was any other information that could help, such as a thankyou letter, or a complaint or an incident or accident sheet completed. She then contacted the local authority to see if there were any new schemes being set up in her area and gathered other local information that might help her with the evaluation process.

Values and principles

Another method that provides an excellent framework for managers to check not only their own attitude and approach, skills and practice, but also the team, the activities and the ethos of their setting, is to use the principles or values that underpin the whole nature of the work. These are laid out in the qualifications of the sector, in Childcare, Early Years and Playwork. The Early Years/Childcare qualifications have ten major principles that give guidelines on how the work with children should be carried out; the Playwork sector has twelve values and assumptions based on the rights of a child to play and have places to play. For more information on these we suggest that you look at one of the books on qualifications given in the Bibliography.

The who? what? why? where? when? method

Who? All teams have a clear responsibility to create opportunities for development, fun, socialising and any number of activities, not just to meet the National Day Care Standards, but to serve the children and young people using the setting. Without an evaluation of how the team is working and how the setting is running, a huge gap in understanding and in creating new opportunities is left open. Evaluation looks at the whole operation together; the learning from this process is invaluable.

Most staff and children are happy to take part in an evaluation process if they understand why it is being done and if suggestions for improvements are taken seriously. Most people will not want to give opinions or comments if they think nothing will change; it makes them feel less valued. So in finding ways that involve everyone, a manager can show staff and children that they are listened to, are valued and do belong.

A setting offering a service to older children and young people may not have much contact, if any, with their parents and families and so including them in the evaluation process would be difficult and perhaps not so necessary.

What? Exactly what you decide to evaluate will depend on the following:

- the aim and objectives of your setting
- what the evaluation process is for, e.g. if it is the first such process, its aim may be to discover how contented the children are with the service and the staff within the setting
- what you are hoping to use the results of the process for
- how it will help improve the service.

Once you have a clear goal for the evaluation exercise, dividing the questions into sections even for yourself can be very useful. If the purpose is not stated and made clear then the evaluation process can lose focus and any good that could be derived from the exercise will be lost.

CASE STUDY

Joanna, manager of a full-day care scheme including an after-school club, wanted to find out about the usage of the new building, the range of activities on offer and what the children and team felt about the building and the programme as a whole. The goal of the evaluation was to use this data as evidence of continual improvements and validations for further funding applications.

She drew up a list of questions for herself that were divided into four sections. The first section covered all the areas of the new building, who used them, when and how often. She also asked if children and staff liked the different areas. The second section looked at the activities on offer; the third section had questions on the outdoor area, usage, likes, etc; and the fourth section had questions on what else the team and the children would like to see happening at the centre. She then looked at how she would get this data from everyone. Questionnaires were all right for staff and could be followed up with a focused team meeting to discuss findings, but the children would not find that method very easy or enjoyable. So she asked the staff to come up with some activities that would get the feedback she wanted from the children. They designed a game where children moved around the room according to their likes and dislikes, one member of staff recording the information, then they took the children to each part of the building and looked at the usage.

Joanna has used a range of methods to get the data she wants, having planned the questions in different sections with the focus being children's and staff opinions on the use of the space.

Why? Settings need to obtain feedback on the service for a variety of reasons:

- To check that each individual child's needs are being met

- To enable children and staff to reflect and comment on different aspects of the programme/service

- To show the children and staff that their opinions are valued and it is their service

- To develop a sense of belonging and responsibility

- To see where there are opportunities to improve the service

- To allow reflection on what has been successful and why, and what has not and why

- To continually monitor practice and quality

- To learn from the feedback given and take pride in praise and be aware of mistakes.

Remember, the principal aim of a full evaluation process is to judge if value has been offered in what the setting does and how it operates, to take into consideration all the successes and the failures, and to look for ways to improve what is offered.

Where? Most evaluations will take place at the setting, but not all. Managers, for instance, may carry out a fuller evaluation of a holiday playscheme after it has taken place somewhere other than the venue for the scheme. This would allow both those who attended the scheme and those who worked there to have more time to reflect on all the aspects before giving their ideas or opinions.

You can be as creative as you like, it is really up to you to decide on the place to carry out an evaluation. Annual General Meetings (AGMs) could be a useful place to hold evaluation processes; other ideas would include summer or winter parties where parents and others come along. Some managers take their teams away from the normal working environment, allowing them to get the benefit of being in a different place and, therefore, an atmosphere which can stimulate greater reflection and discussion.

When? Effective evaluation processes should take place at least once a year, involve as many people as possible and use a variety of methods to gather the information. It is not a quick question-and-answer action that gets looked at once and then locked away in a drawer so the Quality Assurance Action Plan can have a tick by 'Evaluate your service'!

Some settings carry out a mini-evaluation before the summer holidays, when they close, and a full evaluation at the end of the year. Some will carry out a full evaluation process every two years; however, leaving it this length of time does not allow for opportunities to be looked at and needs addressed effectively.

Planning, collecting and analysing data

A manager who plans the evaluation process will get a good return of data in most instances. This part of the exercise may take up some time, especially in reflecting on issues to be included and in simply planning the action points.

Planning
The following points will need to be considered:

- What the goal of the evaluation is
- The range of questions to be asked
- Who is to take part and when
- How the process will work – which methods to use
- What the deadline is or what other time constraints will impact on the exercise
- Who will see the results
- How the results will be used.

Allow a reasonable amount of time for the process to take place if you want it to be successful.

Doing

- Collect information that may be needed, e.g. statistics on how many children come to the setting, their ages and ethnicity, costs, types of activities on offer, accidents and incidents, etc.

- Send out or give out questionnaires, if using this method.

- Brief staff and children about the process.

- Carry out the evaluation process.

Analysis

- Draw up a grid or table to record findings from each evaluation method.

- Study the findings.

- Check you have as much feedback as you need, e.g. if you did a game with a group of children, how many were there?

- Clarify with staff any points or issues that are not clear.

Getting others involved

In addition to the above points you may find that you are encouraging everyone to take on the evaluation process as part of the natural development of the team and the setting. There are suspicions that evaluations are linked to changes that are detrimental to staff, such as redundancies. Of course, that may be necessary in your setting but there are ways of finding out if this is the case other than through a process of gaining and then analysing feedback for the benefit of the setting.

Always get the children involved from the earliest opportunity and regardless of how infrequently they attend the setting.

Questionnaires

The questions need to be very precise. You could ask about likes and dislikes, opinions on certain activities and the meals/snacks, how children relate to staff, how staff relate to them, what they think about the access to the setting, how they feel their views are taken, what they think should happen at certain times of the year, and so on. Do not have too many questions and make sure they are age-appropriate.

Graffiti wall

This is simply a wall that has been covered in plain paper where suggestions and comments can always be written – and read – perhaps with a time limit for it being there so the purpose of it does not get lost in the day-to-day activity of the setting. (Decorators' lining paper is excellent for this.)

Games

Develop a game. It could be a physical one, where children move in the room according to their opinions of the questions asked. A traditional game like this is Vote with Your Feet, where participants are asked what they think about certain topics, issues, etc. and move accordingly. Once you have decided on the questions – do not have too many; the game gets boring – put large pieces of flip chart in several places with possible answers such as Brilliant, Not bad, OK, Poor. The children are asked the questions and asked to run to the area that best represents what they feel.

For the older age group, a board game could be used, with the questions on cards and with counters to move in different directions on a board according to what is working well and what is not.

Art

Pictures can be useful. Groups of children could do a joint picture of what they think are the good and bad points of the setting. They could then be asked questions about the picture to draw out feelings and ideas. In addition, you could provide a large picture of something recognisable like a toy box (remember age appropriateness), and hand out lots of Post-its and pens or, for younger ones, paper copies of toys. The children then put their thoughts on the Post-its or toys and stick them on the picture. Anything that is in the toy box is satisfactory or good, anything outside is not.

Make a 'happy chart' with different sections for the areas you wish to get feedback on and a rating scale. This can be as large as you like. Ask the children to mark on the chart how they would rate the different areas you are evaluating. The onus is then on them to think about the questions and physically mark the chart.

Discussions

Of course, informal discussions with children, with someone noting major comments or main points, can be very useful if the discussion does not go off at a tangent. Recording conversations can be a good way of getting older children involved; it becomes a mini-activity or project that they can take control of. Asking some children to carry this out as a project can result in more participation. Make sure that the equipment is of good quality and there are opportunities for everyone to hear the recording.

Meetings

Don't forget the parents, if you have relationships with them. A formal questionnaire with a letter explaining what you are doing could be used, although the drawback of this method is that not all adults can read or speak English. If this is the case with your catchment area, invite them in for an informal meeting or a parent/carer event, such as a summer party, and ask them the questions.

Successes and failures

All settings have them – successes and failures. It helps to look at both and really check the findings. By this we mean mentally, and possibly verbally, check with others that what has been considered a failure is in fact a failure. It is also important to put into action suggestions that are relevant and achievable. Children, when asked about activities and what new ones they would like to see at their setting, often put ones that in reality are just not possible due to space and budget.

Nevertheless this needs to be addressed in some way with them; a gentle clear explanation as to what is possible and what is not should be given.

It is very important to note successes and share them. By sharing the results, especially the good points, staff will be more motivated and feel a sense of satisfaction. For children it develops the sense of belonging, or being valued as part of an important process of the setting that they have come to know. So managers should not keep the findings to themselves; let staff and children see them, so all can experience the 'feel good factor'.

Putting it into practice

- Think ahead: when is the best time to carry out an evaluation process for your setting?

- Look at what areas/issues have been coming up in team meetings that might need to be included or need a fuller exploration.

- Give plenty of warning to the team that this process is going to happen and explain what the purpose of it is.

- Ask children to be involved, and be creative in arranging ways for them to do so.

- Plan your evaluation: think about what needs to be asked and why.

- Give clear deadlines for replies or data to be collected by.

- Once all data is collected allow yourself, and/or the team, time to read and discuss the information to make a proper analysis.

- Record the data and summarise it in a report that can be circulated to everyone – don't forget to inform the children of the findings.

- Look at ways of acting upon the findings in the setting.

Contact list

Action for Leisure   tel. 01926 650195   www.actionforleisure.org.uk
An organisation that offers advice, information and training for those who work
and live with children with a disability; produces a quarterly magazine full of ideas.

Children's Legal Centre   tel. 01206 872466 (administration and publications),
01206 873820 (advice)   www.essex.ac.uk/clc/
Advice, information and news sheets on how law affects and relates to children.

Children's Play Council   tel. 020 7843 6016   www.ncb.org.uk/cpc/
An organisation that aims to raise the importance of play in children's lives by
working with, and advising, other organisations, government and policymakers;
produces *Playtoday*, a free news sheet on play.

Children's Play Information Service   tel. 020 7843 6303
www.ncb.org.uk/library/cpis/
An information resource service specialising in children's play.

Common Threads Training Ltd   tel. 07000 785215
www.commonthreads.co.uk
Provides training, including management skills training, for adults working with
children in out-of-school settings.

Community Insight   tel. 01793 512612   www.c-insight.demon.co.uk
An organisation that sells books and resources for trainers and practitioners in
childcare, education and playwork.

Freeplay Network   tel. 01482 474611   www.freeplaynetwork.org.uk
Aims to give advice, information and support to anyone providing, or wishing to
provide, free play.

Furzeham Graphics   tel. 01803 850157
A private firm producing resources for playwork qualifications.

GIZMO Resources   tel. 01274 616126   www.gizmo.co.uk
Produces resources for people working with children.

ILAM (Institute for Leisure and Management)   tel. 01491 874800
www.ilam.co.uk
Very much involved in promoting play through leisure; produces resources and
has a members' magazine.

Institute of Personnel Management and Development   tel. 020 8971 9000
www.ipd.co.uk
Supports and promotes management, personnel and training, has a large membership and is an awarding body for some qualifications.

Institute of Reflective Practice   tel. 01452 731177
www.reflectivepractices.com
Publishes journals and articles and promotes the use of Reflective Practice in the workplace.

Kidsactive   tel. 020 7736 4443   www.kidsactive.org.uk
An organisation that runs adventure playgrounds for children with a disability, offers training in working with children and produces a quarterly magazine.

KIDSCAPE   tel. 020 7730 3300   www.educate.co.uk/bull2.htm
An organisation that researches, lobbies and provides resources on bullying, child protection and generally keeping safe.

Kids Club Network   tel. 020 7512 2112   www.kidsclub.com
An organisation that supports and promotes out-of-school childcare for playworkers; also has a quality assurance scheme and many other resources.

Letterbox Library   tel. 020 7503 4801   www.letterboxlibrary.com
Specialists in non-sexist and multicultural books for children.

National Children's Bureau   tel. 020 7843 6000   www.ncb.org.uk
A national organisation that supports, researches, lobbies and advises on all aspects of children's lives; produces a members' magazine, updates; holds conferences and houses a good library of books and journals relating to work, development and care of children and young people.

National Playing Fields Association   tel. 020 7833 5360   www.npfa.co.uk
An organisation that specifically supports the use and improvement of playing fields, playing spaces and playgrounds for **all** children.

National Qualifications Framework (NQF)
www.qca.org.uk/nq/subjects/childcare/
Part of QCA's remit; has all the qualifications in childcare, old and new.

National Society for the Prevention of Cruelty to Children (NSPCC)
tel. 020 7825 2500   www.nspcc.org.uk
Produces literature relevant to working with children and a range of training courses.

Nursery World   tel. 020 7782 3000   www.nursery-world.co.uk
Produces a weekly magazine and other services.

Playlink   tel. 020 7820 3800   www.playlink.org.uk
A play organisation supporting children's play through publications, projects, support of local play service providers, conferences, training and lobbying.

Playwords   tel. 07000 785215   email: playwords@commonthreads.co.uk
A magazine produced six times a year for all those involved in children's play; published by Common Threads Publications Ltd.

Bibliography

Adair, J. (2002) *100 Greatest Ideas for Effective Leadership and Management*. Oxford: Capstone.

Back, K. and Back, K. (1992) *Assertiveness at Work*, 2nd edn. Maidenhead: McGraw-Hill.

Belbin, R. M. (1995) *Team Roles at Work*. London: Butterworth Heinemann.

Berne, E. (1964) *Games People Play: The Psychology of Human Relationships*. Harmondsworth: Penguin Books.

Blanchard, K. (1994) *Leadership and the One Minute Manager*. London: Harper Collins Business.

Cavanagh, M. (2002) *Against Equality of Opportunity*. Oxford: Clarendon Press.

Childcare and Early Years, 12, Spring 2002. London: Kids Club Network with the Department for Education and Skills.

Children's Play Council (1999) *The New Charter for Children's Play*. London: National Children's Bureau.

Clemments, P. and Spinks, T. (2000) *The Equal Opportunities Handbook*, 3rd edn. London: Kogan Page.

Dickson, A. (1982) *A Woman in Your Own Right: Assertiveness and You*. London: Quartet Books.

Fisher, R. and Ury, W. (1981) *Getting to Yes: Negotiating Agreement without Giving in*. London: Arrow.

Guillebeaux, J. (2002) 'More is caught than taught'. *Inspire Conference*. London.

Heller, R. and Hindle, T. (1998) *Essential Managers' Manual*. London: Dorling Kindersley.

Hersey, P. (1984) *The Situational Leader*. Chichester: John Wiley & Son.

Hopson, B. and Scally. M. (1999) *Build Your Own Rainbow*. Chalford: Management Books.

Hughes, B. (2001) *Evolutionary Playwork and Reflective Analytic Practice*. London: Routledge.

Jay, R. (2000) *Build a Great Team*. London: Prentice-Hall.

Johnson, D. W. and Johnson, F. P. (1975) *Joining Together: Group Theory and Group Skills*, 7th edn. Boston, MA: Allyn and Bacon.

Kapasi, H. (2002) *Playing in Parallel: A Study of Access to Play Provision by Black and Minority Children in London*. London Play.

Landsberg, M. (2003) *Tao of Motivation*. London: Profile Books.

Lindenfield, G. (1986) *Assert Yourself*. London: Thorsons.

Lindon, J. (2001) *Understanding Children's Play*. London: National Children's Bureau.

Malik, H. (1998) *A Practical Guide to Equal Opportunities*. Cheltenham: Stanley Thornes.

Markham, U. (1996) *Managing Conflict: How to Deal with Difficult Situations at Work*. London: Thorsons.

Philpot, T. (ed.) (1999) *Political Correctness and Social Work*. London: IEA Health and Welfare.

PIP Guidelines Series 1 (2002) *It Doesn't Just Happen*. London: Kidsactive.

Pocket Oxford English Dictionary (7th edn 1984). Oxford: Clarendon Press.

Kimball Fisher, *et al.* (1995) *Tips for Teams: A Ready Reference for Solving Common Team Problems*. New York: McGraw-Hill.

Smith, A. and Langston, A. (1999) *Managing Staff in Early Years Settings*. London: Routledge.

Stobbart, T. (ed.) (2002) *Take Ten More for Play*. Furzeham Graphics and the National Centre for Playwork Education, South West.

Tassoni, P. (1998) *Childcare and Education*. Oxford: Heinemann.

Tassoni, P. (2001) *Playwork Level 3, Candidate Handbook*. Oxford: Heinemann.

Taylor, G. (1999) *Managing Conflict*. London: Directory of Social Change.

Printed in the United Kingdom
by Lightning Source UK Ltd.
124938UK00006B/7-10/A